Front cover
Mértola Mosque, Mértola

Museum With No Frontiers *Exhibition Trails*

ISLAMIC ART IN THE MEDITERRANEAN | **PORTUGAL**

In the Lands of the Enchanted Moorish Maiden
Islamic Art in Portugal

Museum With No Frontiers

EUROPEAN UNION
MEDA-Euromed Heritage
European Social Fund

The MWNF Exhibition Trail *IN THE LANDS OF THE ENCHANTED MOORISH MAIDEN: Islamic Art in Portugal* is part of the international cycle *Islamic Art in the Mediterranean*. Its realisation within the framework of the "Gateway to the Mediterranean" project was co-financed by the European Union through the Pilot Scheme for Co-operation between Spain, Portugal and Morocco, in accordance with article 10 of the European Regional Development Fund (ERDF). With the support of:

Ministério da Economia
MINISTRY OF THE ECONOMY, PORTUGAL

Office of the Secretary of State for Tourism, Portugal

The Exhibition Trail was developed by the Cultural Tourism Growth Programme, with the support of the Portuguese Directorate-General for Tourism and was co-financed by the Portuguese Institute for Tourism Funding and Support.

First edition
© 2001 Cultural Tourism Growth Programme, Lisbon, Portugal & Museum With No Frontiers (texts and illustrations)
© 2001 Electa (Grijalbo Mondadori S.A.), Madrid, Spain & Museum With No Frontiers

Second edition
© 2010 Campo Arqueológico de Mértola, Portugal & Museum With No Frontiers (texts and illustrations)
© 2010 Museum With No Frontiers

ISBN: 978-3-902782-12-0

All rights reserved.

Information
www.museumwnf.org
www.mwnfbooks.net

Museum With No Frontiers
Idea and overall concept
Eva Schubert

Head of the Project
Flávio Lopes, Lisbon

Curatorial Committee
Cláudio Torres, Mértola
Santiago Macias, Mértola
Susana Gómez, Mértola

Catalogue

Introductions
Cláudio Torres
Santiago Macias

Presentation of the Itineraries
Curatorial Committee

as well as with the collaboration of the following authors
Artur Goulart de Melo Borges, Évora
Cristina Garcia, Lisbon
Fernando Branco Correia, Évora
Isabel Cristina F. Fernandes, Palmela
Maria Adelaide Miranda, Lisbon
Maria João Vieira, Serpa
Maria Regina Anacleto, Coimbra
Mário Pereira, Lisbon
Miguel Rego, Barrancos
Paula Noronha, Faro
Ruben de Carvalho, Lisbon

Technical texts
Maria José Machado Santos, Lisbon

Translation
John Elliott, Lisbon

Editing
Mandi Gomez, London

Photographer
António Cunha, Beja

General map and sketches
José Russo, Lisbon

General introduction
Islamic Art in the Mediterranean

Text
Jamila Binous, Tunis
Mahmoud Hawari, East-Jerusalem
Manuela Marín, Madrid
Gönül Öney, Izmir

Plans
Şakir Çakmak, Izmir
Ertan Daş, Izmir
Yekta Demiralp, Izmir

Layout and design
Augustina Fernández,
Electa España, Madrid
Christian Eckart,
MWNF, Vienna (2nd edition)

Local coordination

Cultural Heritage
Teresa Gamboa, Lisbon

Legal
Isabel Menezes, Lisbon

Cultural promotion and events co-ordination
Elsa Peralta, Lisbon

Field checks
Miguel Valdemar, Mértola

International coordination

Overall coordination
Eva Schubert

Curatorial committees, translations, editing and production of the catalogues (1st edition)
Sakina Missoum, Madrid

Acknowledgements

The Cultural Tourism Growth Programme and Museum With No Frontiers wish to express their gratitude to the following organisations for helping to make this project possible:

City Councils of
Landroal, Albufeira, Alcácer do Sal, Alcoutim, Alenquer, Aljezur, Alter do Chão, Arganil, Barrancos, Beja, Castelo de Vide, Castro Marim, Coimbra, Crato, Elvas, Évora, Faro, Idanha-a-Nova, Lagoa, Lisbon, Loulé, Marvão, Mértola, Monchique, Moura, Óbidos, Oliveira do Hospital, Ourique, Palmela, Penacova, Sabugal, Santarém, Serpa, Sesimbra, Silves, Sintra, Tavira, Vila do Bispo, Vila Real de Santo António, Vila Viçosa; Comisión Municipal de Turismo de Sintra, Comisión Municipal de Turismo de Elvas, Confederación de Turismo, Dirección General de Edificios y Monumentos Nacionales, EBAHL (Equipamientos de los Barrios Históricos de Lisboa).
Thanks also to the following organisations: Pousadas de Portugal, Fondo de Turismo, ICEP (Instituto de Comercio Exterior de Portugal), Instituto de Archivos Nacionales / Torre do Tombo, Instituto Portugués de las Artes y del Espectáculo, Instituto Portugués de Museos, Instituto Portugués del Patrimonio Arquitectónico, Región de Turismo del Algarve, Región de Turismo del Centro, Región de Turismo de Évora, Región de Turismo de la Planicie Dourada, Región de Turismo de Ribatejo, Región de Turismo de São Mamede, Región de Turismo de Setúbal (Costa Azul), Turismo de Lisboa.

The Portuguese organisers and MWNF would also like to thank their associates in the project "A way into the Mediterranean" for the scientific and technical support they have received:

Ministry of Education, Culture and Sport of Spain, General Directorates of Fine Arts,
   Cultural Heritage, and of Cultural Co-operation and Communication
Ministry of Cultural Affairs, Morocco
Ministry of Tourism, National Office for Tourism, Morocco

Photographic references
See page 5, as well as:
Ann & Peter Jousiffe (London), page 20 (Aleppo Citadel).
Archivos Oronoz Fotógrafos (Madrid), page 23 (Alhambra, Granada).

Plan references
Ettinghaussen, R., and Grabar, O. (Madrid, I, 1997), page 26 (Damascus Mosque).
Sönmez, Z. (Ankara, 1995), page 27 (Divriği and Istanbul Mosques) and page 28 (Sivas Mosque).
Viguera, S. (Madrid), page 28 (Minaret types).
Blair, S. S, and Bloom, J. M. (Madrid, II, 1999), page 29 (Sultan Hassan Mosque and Madrasa).
Ettinghaussen, R., and Grabar, O. (Madrid, I, 1997), page 30 (Qasr al-Khayr al-Sharqi).
Kuran, A. (Istanbul, 1986), page 31 (Sultan Khan Aksaray).

Produced within the framework of the European Union's Euro-Mediterranean cooperation programme, MEDA-Euromed Heritage Programme.

Preface

In 1996 Museum With No Frontiers (MWNF) initiated a comprehensive programme to research, document and increase knowledge and public awareness of the history and cultural legacy of Islam in the countries surrounding the Mediterranean basin. This book is one of the outcomes of this programme, which involves hundreds of scholars and is carried out in cooperation with institutions from all the countries concerned. Important initial funding from the European Union made it possible to set the basis for a sustainable network of public and private partners implementing attractive projects in the field of culture, education and tourism.

When the MWNF programme was first launched, the topic of Islamic art and architecture was familiar only to experts and there was an implicit understanding that cultural heritage in the Mediterranean meant the legacy of the classical civilisations. Thanks to the launch coinciding with the establishment at the end of 1995 of the Euro-Mediterranean Partnership, a joint initiative of the European Union and its Mediterranean neighbours, the MWNF programme took off quickly and became a pioneering venture to disseminate knowledge about the world contribution of Islam.

The initial focus on the Mediterranean region was determined by its place at the centre stage of Islamic history and the economic and cultural interdependence of its shores throughout that history. However, we look forward to extending the programme to other areas of the Islamic and Arab world.

In connection with our Exhibition Trails and related thematic guides, MWNF also offers the possibility to participate in themed tours organised in cooperation with specialised local travel agencies in each country. For further details and virtual tours to the Exhibition Trails please visit *www.mwnftravels.net*.

Our Virtual Museum – *www.discoverislamicart.org* – offers access to a large collection of Islamic artefacts and monuments, with descriptions for all items regularly updated in Arabic, English, French and Spanish. A series of Virtual Exhibitions enables visitors to locate the topics of the Exhibition Trails within the relevant regional context.

All MWNF publications are compiled, written and illustrated by scholars and photographers from the country concerned and convey the cultural and historical context of the featured sites from a local perspective. 'We appreciate only what we see and we understand only what we know.' It was with this idea in mind that our Egyptian colleagues who designed the visit and wrote the text for this book paid particular attention to providing information that usually remains undisclosed to tourists.

On behalf of the whole MWNF team I wish you an enjoyable visit to Islamic Portugal and look forward to meeting you soon in another part of our Euro-Mediterranean museum with no frontiers.

Eva Schubert
Chairperson and CEO
Museum With No Frontiers

Some preliminary words

The *IN THE LANDS OF THE ENCHANTED MOORISH MAIDEN: Islamic Art in Portugal* Exhibition Trail is the first production of the Cultural Tourism Growth Programme, set up by the Portuguese government in 1997. The programme is a fundamental part of the government's objectives for increasing the quality of tourism and improving the image of Portugal, thereby bringing both direct and indirect benefits to the national economy.

This genuine "exhibition" spreads across the central and southern regions of present-day Portugal – the Gharb al-Andalus of Islamic times – and presents to a vast public the historical and artistic remains of roughly five centuries of Muslim presence, much of which is still relatively unknown, even to local inhabitants.

The successful implementation of this project was only possible thanks to the joint efforts of various sectors of the government, in particular those of tourism and culture, the support of the various municipalities, and the participation of countless public and private entities. The prime motivation for this programme is that it should contribute to the social, cultural and economic development of the respective local communities, enhancing both their environment and heritage through tourism.

The aim of opening up our heritage to an international public who are increasingly curious about our country, is thoroughly achieved with the characteristics of this Exhibition Trail: an initiative that forms part of the Museum With No Frontiers programme and is devoted to the theme of *Islamic Art in the Mediterranean*.

Flávio Lopes
Director
Cultural Tourism Growth Programme

Advice

Transliteration of the Arabic

We have retained the common spelling for Arabic words in common use and included those in the English dictionary, such as "mihrab". For all other words, we have simplified the transcription. We do not transcribe the initial *hamza* or the *'ayn*, nor do we differentiate between short and long vowels, which are written as *a, i, ou*. For example, *ta' marbuta* is transcribed by *a* (absolute state followed by a genitive).

Some of the proper nouns are transliterated in the text according to the Oxford Dictionary. The transcription for the 28 Arabic consonants are provided in the table below:

ء	'	ح	h	ز	z	ط	t	ق	q	ه	h
ب	b	خ	kh	س	s	ظ	z	ك	k	و	u/w
ت	t	د	d	ش	sh	ع	'	ل	l	ي	y/i
ث	th	ذ	d/h	ص	s	غ	g/h	م	m		
ج	j	ر	r	ض	d	ف	f	ن	n		

Words in italics in the text without an accompanying translation can be found in the glossary. Some words, however, remain in Roman for ease of reading but also can be found in the glossary. These are: Moorish, Mudejar, Mozarab and villa, although *villae* is italicised.

The Muslim era

The Muslim era began with the exodus of the prophet Muhammad from Mecca to Yathrib. Then the name was changed to *Madina*, "the City" or "town of the Prophet". With his small community of followers (70 people and members of his family) recently converted to Islam, the Prophet undertook the *al-hijra* (literally "the emigration") and the new era began.

The date of the emigration is the first of the month of *Muharram* in year 1 of the *Hijra*, which corresponds to the 16th July of the year 622 of the Christian era. The Muslim year is made up of twelve lunar months, each month having 29 or 30 days. Thirty years form a cycle in which the 2nd, 5th, 7th, 10th, 13th, 16th, 18th, 21st, 24th, 26th and 29th are leap years having 355 days; the others are normal years with 354 days. The Muslim lunar year is 10 or 11 days shorter than the Christian solar year. Each day begins immediately after sunset, i.e. at dusk rather than after midnight. Most Muslim countries use both the *Hijra* Calendar (which indicates all the religious events) and the Christian Calendar.

Dates

Dates are given according to the *Hijra* calendar followed by their equivalent date on the Christian Calendar after an oblique stroke. The *Hijra* date is not indicated in references derived from Christian sources, European historical events, those occurring in Europe, Christian Dynasties and dates after 1250, the year which marked the end of the Muslim period in the west of the Iberian peninsula (*Gharb al-Andalus*).
Exact correspondence between years in one calendar and another is only possible when the day and month are given. To facilitate reading, we chose to avoid intermediate years and, in the case of *Hijra* dates falling between the beginning and the end of a century, the two centuries are mentionned.

Abbreviations:
e = end; b = beginning; d = dead; f.h. = first half; s.h. = second half; m = middle.

Practical advice

The *IN THE LANDS OF THE ENCHANTED MOORISH MAIDEN: Islamic Art in Portugal* Exhibition Trail is subdivided into ten itineraries, each of which represents a specific geographical area. Each itinerary lasts one or two days and is designed to enhance the cultural heritage and the environmental and historical resources of the respective region. The itineraries include the main route and alternative routes, as well as "highlights" which describe complementary features (the title is shown in bold letters against a yellow background), natural features and landscapes chosen for their particular interest and legends associated with selected places are in italics against a grey background.

The various stages (marked with Arabic numerals) of each itinerary (marked with Roman numerals) are accompanied by information of a technical nature (opening times, whether or not guided visits are possible, etc.), whilst suggestions are given as to the most suitable route for getting to the monument in italics.

Each itinerary is shown in picture form, which enables visitors to immediately see it as a whole, as well as showing the journeys that will be necessary to complete it. The optional routes (shown in grey) include those monuments that may take longer to visit than the time allotted to the itinerary, either for reasons of geographical distance or because of the great wealth of the main itinerary.

Some monuments were not open to visitors at the time this catalogue was printed. Visitors are strongly advised to check the accuracy of the information provided before they begin their journey.

It should be remembered that on Sundays and Saints' days, religious services are held at many churches. Visitors are therefore asked to time their visit so that, if possible, they do not coincide with the times of worship.

Museum With No Frontiers cannot be held responsible for any incidents that may occur during your visit to the exhibition.

Translator's note

An attempt has been made to respect the names of sites and monuments, whenever these are considered to be established names. For example: "Arco do Miradeiro" (Itinerary IV), although reference is also made to places such as "Alandroal Castle" (Itinerary IV). Where possible, the name of the monument has been translated and placed in brackets after the name in Portuguese whenever this seems relevant, e.g. Castelo de São Jorge (St. George's Castle).
In the case of kings and queens, the normal Portuguese designation of D. has been used and the name of the monarch has been kept in Portuguese (e.g. D. Fernando II), although Castilian kings and queens are mentioned without any specific title.

INDEX

15 **Islamic Art in the Mediterranean**
Jamila Binous, Mahmoud Hawari, Manuela Marín, Gönül Öney

35 **Gharb al-Andalus: A Brief History**
Santiago Macias

40 **The Far West of Iberia**
Cláudio Torres

45 **Itinerary I**
Mudejar Art
Cláudio Torres, Santiago Macias, Maria Regina Anacleto, Cristina Garcia, Paula Noronha
Fado
Ruben de Carvalho

67 **Itinerary II**
Between Moors and Mozarabs
Cláudio Torres, Maria Adelaide Miranda, Mário Pereira, Santiago Macias
The Lorvão Apocalypse
Maria Adelaide Miranda

79 **Itinerary III**
Idanha: Border Country
Cláudio Torres, Mário Pereira, Cristina Garcia, Paula Noronha

93 **Itinerary IV**
The Road to the Gharb
Cláudio Torres, Santiago Macias, Fernando Branco Correia, Artur Goulart de Melo Borges

105 **Itinerary V**
A Taifa Kingdom: Mértola
Santiago Macias, Cláudio Torres, Miguel Rego, Maria João Vieira
Weaving Workshops
Santiago Macias

127 **Itinerary VI**
Guadiana: The Great Southern River
Santiago Macias, Cláudio Torres, Cristina Garcia, Paula Noronha

137 **Itinerary VII**
Between the Algarve and the Mountains
Santiago Macias

153 **Itinerary VIII**
Silves: The Capital of Almohad Art
Santiago Macias, Cláudio Torres

163 **Itinerary IX**
The Headland at the World's End
Cláudio Torres, Cristina Garcia, Paula Noronha

171 **Itinerary X**
The Castles of the River Sado
Cláudio Torres, Isabel Cristina F. Fernandes, Cristina Garcia, Paula Noronha

181 **Glossary**

185 **Historical Events**

189 **Further Reading**

193 **Authors**

ISLAMIC DYNASTIES IN THE MEDITERRANEAN

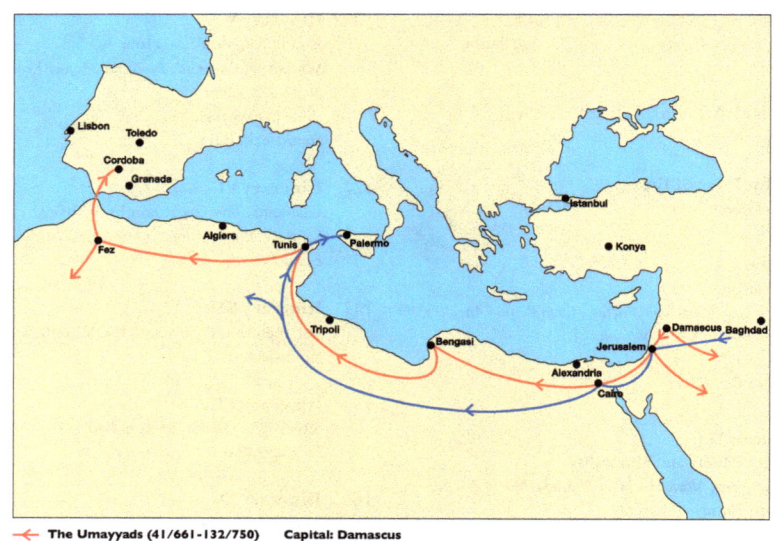

← The Umayyads (41/661-132/750)   Capital: Damascus
← The Abbasids (132/750-656/1258)   Capital: Baghdad

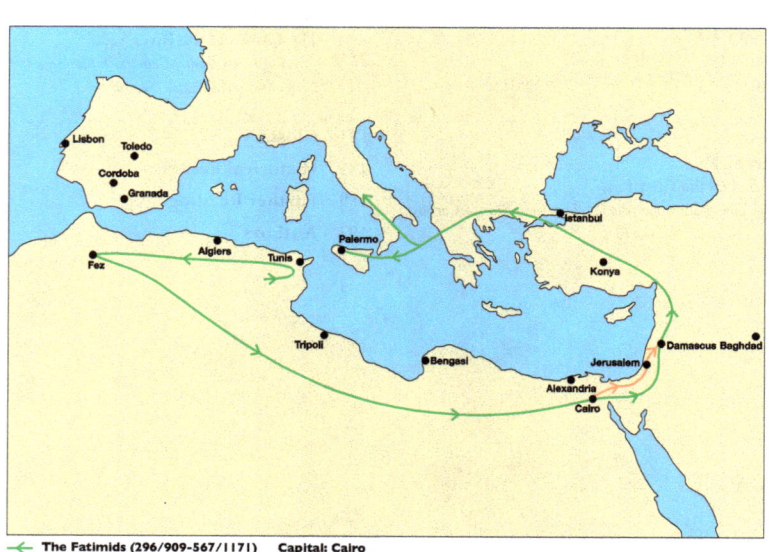

← The Fatimids (296/909-567/1171)   Capital: Cairo
← The Mamluks (648/1250-923/1517)   Capital: Cairo

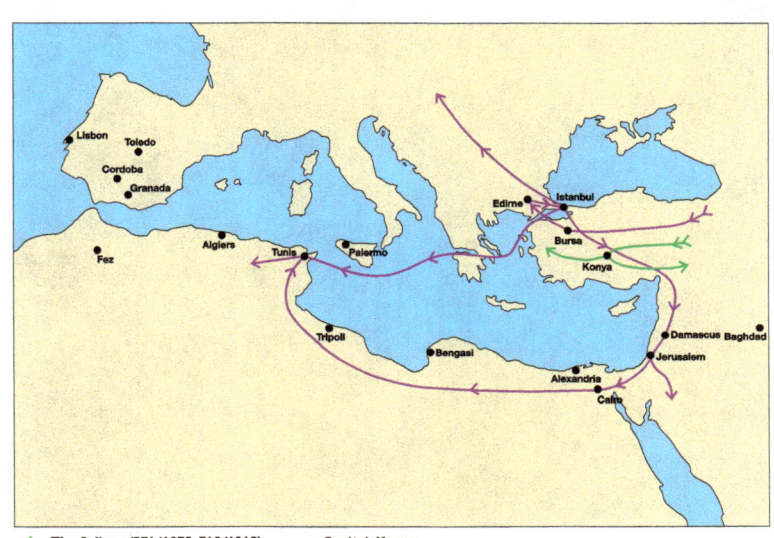

← The Seljuqs (571/1075-718/1318)   Capital: Konya
← The Ottomans (699/1299-1340/1922)   Capital: Istanbul

← The Almoravids (427/1036-541/1147)   Capital: Marrakesh
← The Almohads (515/1121-667/1269)   Capital: Marrakesh

Qusayr 'Amra, mural in
the Audience Hall,
Badiya of Jordan.

ISLAMIC ART IN THE MEDITERRANEAN

Jamila Binous
Mahmoud Hawari
Manuela Marín
Gönül Öney

The Legacy of Islam in the Mediterranean

Since the first half of the 1st/7th century, the history of the Mediterranean Basin has belonged, in remarkably similar proportion, to two cultures, Islam and the Christian West. This extensive history of conflict and contact has created a mythology that is widely diffused in the collective imagination, a mythology based on the image of the other as the unyielding enemy, strange and alien, and as such, incomprehensible. It is of course true that battles punctuated those centuries from the time when the Muslims spilled forth from the Arabian Peninsula and took possession of the Fertile Crescent, Egypt, and later, North Africa, Sicily, and the Iberian Peninsula, penetrating into Western Europe as far as the south of France. At the beginning of the 2nd/8th century, the Mediterranean came under Islamic control.

This drive to expand, of an intensity seldom equalled in human history, was carried out in the name of a religion that considered itself then heir to its two immediate antecedents: Judaism and Christianity. It would be a gross oversimplification to explain the Islamic expansion exclusively in religious terms. One widespread image in the West presents Islam as a religion of simple dogmas adapted to the needs of the common people, spread by vulgar warriors who poured out from the desert bearing the *Qur'an* on the blades of their swords. This coarse image does away with the intellectual complexity of a religious message that transformed the world from the moment of its inception. It identifies this message with a military threat, and thus justifies a response on the same terms. Finally, it reduces an entire culture to only one of its elements, religion, and in doing so, deprives it of the potential for evolution and change.

The Mediterranean countries that were progressively incorporated into the Muslim world began their journeys from very different starting points. Forms of Islamic life that began to develop in each were quite logically different within the unity that resulted from their shared adhesion to the new religious dogma. It is precisely the capacity to assimilate elements of previous cultures (Hellenistic, Roman, etc.), which has been one of the defining characteristics of Islamic societies. If one restricts one's observations to the geographical area of the Mediterranean, which was extremely diverse culturally at the time of the emergence of Islam, one will discern quickly that this initial moment does not represent a break with previous history in the least. One comes to realise that it is impossible to imagine a monolithic and immutable Islamic world, blindly following an inalterable religious message.

If anything can be singled out as the *leitmotiv* running through the area of the Mediterranean, it is diversity of expression combined with harmony of sentiment, a sentiment more cultural than religious. In the Iberian Peninsula – to begin with the western perimeter of the Mediterranean – the presence of Islam, initially brought about by military conquest, produced a society clearly differentiated from, but in permanent contact with Christian society. The importance of the cultural expression of this Islamic society was felt even after it ceased to exist as such, and gave rise to perhaps one of the most original components of Spanish culture, Mudejar art. Portugal maintained strong Mozarab traditions throughout the Islamic period and there are many imprints from this time that are still clearly visible today. In Morocco and Tunisia, the legacy of al-Andalus was assimilated into the local forms and continues to be evident to this day. The western Mediterranean produced original forms of expression that reflected its conflicting and plural historical evolution.

Lodged between East and West, the Mediterranean Sea is endowed with terrestrial enclaves, such as Sicily, that represent centuries-old key historical locations. Conquered by the Arabs established in Tunisia, Sicily has continued to perpetuate the cultural and historical memory of Islam long after the Muslims ceased to have any political presence on the island. The presence of Sicilian-Norman aesthetic forms preserved in architectural monuments clearly demonstrates that the history of these regions cannot be explained without an understanding of the diversity of social, economic and cultural experiences that flourished on their soil.

In sharp contrast, then, to the immutable and constant image alluded to at the outset, the history of Mediterranean Islam is characterised by surprising diversity. It is made up of a mixture of peoples and ethnicities, deserts and fertile lands. As the major religion has been Islam since the early Middle Ages, it is also true that religious minorities have maintained a presence historically. The Classical Arabic language of the *Qur'an,* has coexisted side-by-side with other languages, as well as with other dialects of Arabic. Within a setting of undeniable unity (Muslim religion, Arabic language and culture), each society has evolved and responded to the challenges of history in its own characteristic manner.

The Emergence and Development of Islamic Art

Throughout these countries, with ancient and diverse civilisations, a new art permeated with images from the Islamic faith emerged at the end of the $2^{nd}/8^{th}$ century, which successfully imposed itself in a period of less than 100 years. This art, in its own particular manner, gave rise to creations and innovations based on unifying regional formulas and architectural and decorative processes, and was simultaneously inspired by the artistic traditions that proceeded it: Greco-Roman and Byzantine, Sasanian, Visigothic, Berber or even Central Asian.

The initial aim of Islamic art was to serve the needs of religion and various aspects of socio-economic life. New buildings appeared for religious purposes such as mosques and sanctuaries. For this reason, architecture played a central role in Islamic art because a whole series of other arts are dependent on it. Apart from architecture a whole range of complimentary minor arts found their artistic expressions in a variety of materials, such as wood, pottery, metal, glass, textiles and paper. In pottery, a great variety of glaze techniques were employed and among these distinguished groups are the lustre and polychrome painted wares. Glass of great beauty was manufactured, reaching excellence with the type adorned with gold and bright enamel colours. In metal work, the most sophisticated technique is inlaying bronze with silver or copper. High-quality textiles and carpets, with geometric, animal and human designs, were made. Illuminated manuscripts with miniature paintings represent a spectacular achievement in the arts of the book. These types of minor arts serve to attest the brilliance of Islamic art.

Figurative art, however, is excluded from the Islamic liturgical domain, which means it is ostracised from the central core of Islamic civilisation and that it is tolerated only at its periphery. Relief work is rare in the decoration of monuments and sculptures are almost flat. This deficit is compensated with a richness in ornamentation on the lavish carved plaster panelling, sculpted wooden panelling, wall tiling and glazed mosaics, as well as on the stalactite friezes, or *muqarnas*. Decorative elements taken from nature, such as leaves, flowers and branches, are generally stylised to the extreme and are so complicated that they rarely call to mind their sources of origin. The intertwining and combining of geometric motifs such as rhombus and etiolated polygons, form interlacing networks that completely cover the surface, resulting in shapes often called arabesques. One innovation within the decorative repertoire is the introduction of epigraphic elements

Dome of the Rock, Jerusalem.

in the ornamentation of monuments, furniture and various other objects. Muslim craftsmen made use of the beauty of Arabic calligraphy, the language of the sacred book, the *Qur'an*, not only for the transcription of the Qur'anic verses, but in all of its variations simply as a decorative motif for the ornamentation of stucco panelling and the edges of panels.

Art was also at the service of rulers. It was for patrons that architects built palaces, mosques, schools, hospitals, bathhouses, *caravanserais* and mausoleums, which would sometimes bear their names. Islamic art is, above all, dynastic art. Each one contributed tendencies that would bring about a partial or complete renewal of artistic forms, depending on historical conditions, the prosperity enjoyed by their states, and the traditions of each people. Islamic art, in spite of its relative unity, allowed for a diversity that gave rise to different styles, each one identified with a dynasty.

The Umayyad Dynasty (41/661-132/750), which transferred the capital of the caliphate to Damascus, represents a singular achievement in the history of Islam. It absorbed and incorporated the Hellenistic and Byzantine legacy in such a way that the classical tradition of the Mediterranean was recast in a new and innovative mould. Islamic art, thus, was formed in Syria, and the architecture, unmistakably Islamic due to the personality of the founders, would continue to bear a relation to Hellenistic and Byzantine art as well. The most important of these monuments are the Dome of the Rock in Jerusalem, the earliest existing monumental Islamic sanctuary, the Great Mosque of Damascus, which served as a model for later mosques, and the desert palaces of Syria, Jordan and Palestine.

Islamic Art in the Mediterranean

When the Abbasid caliphate (132/ 750-656/1258) succeeded the Umayyads, the political centre of Islam was moved from the Mediterranean to Baghdad in Mesopotamia. This factor would influence the development of Islamic civilisation and the entire range of culture, and art would bear the mark of that change. Abbasid art and architecture were influenced by three major traditions: Sassanian, Central Asian and Seljuq. Central Asian influence was already present in Sassanian architecture, but at Samarra this influence is represented by the stucco style with its arabesque ornamentation that would rapidly spread throughout the Islamic world. The influence of Abbasid monuments can be observed in the buildings constructed during this period in the other regions of the empire, particularly Egypt and Ifriqiya. In Cairo, the Mosque of Ibn Tulun (262/876-265/879) is a masterpiece, remarkable for its plan and unity of conception. It was modelled after the Abbasid Great Mosque of Samarra, particularly its spiral minaret. In Kairouan, the capital of Ifriqiya, vassals of the Abbasid caliphs, the Aghlabids (184/800-296/909) expanded the Great Mosque of Kairouan, one of the most venerable congregational mosques in the Maghrib. Its *mihrab* was covered by ceramic tiles from Mesopotamia.

Kairouan Mosque, mihrab, Tunisia.

Kairouan Mosque, minaret, Tunisia.

Citadel of Aleppo, view of the entrance, Syria. *Complex of Qaluwun, Cairo, Egypt.*

The reign of the Fatimids (297/909-567/1171) represents a remarkable period in the history of the Islamic countries of the Mediterranean: North Africa, Sicily, Egypt and Syria. Of their architectural constructions, a few examples remain that bear witness to their past glory. In the central Maghrib the Qal'a of the Bani Hammad and the Mosque of Mahdiya; in Sicily, the Cuba (*Qubba*) and the Zisa (*al-'Aziza*) in Palermo, constructed by Fatimid craftsmen under the Norman King William II; in Cairo, the Azhar Mosque is the most prominent example of Fatimid architecture in Egypt.

The Ayyubids (567/1171-648/1250), who overthrew the Fatimid Dynasty in Cairo, were important patrons of architecture. They established religious institutions *(madrasas, khanqas)* for the propagation of *Sunni* Islam, mausoleums and welfare projects, as well as awesome fortifications pertaining to the military conflict with the Crusaders. The Citadel of Aleppo in Syria is a remarkable example of their military architecture.

The Mamluks (648/1250-923/1517) successors of the Ayyubids, successfully resisted the Crusades and the Mongols, achieved the unity of Syria and Egypt and created a formidable empire. The wealth and luxury of the Mamluk Sultan's court in Cairo motivated artists and architects to achieve an extraordinarily elegant style of architecture. For the world of Islam, the Mamluk period marked a rebirth and renaissance. The enthusiasm for establishing religious foundations and reconstructing existing ones place the Mamluks among the greatest patrons of art and architecture in the history of Islam. The Mosque of Hassan (757/1356), a funerary mosque built with a cruciform plan in which the four arms of the cross were formed by four *iwan*s of the building around a central courtyard, was typical of the era. Anatolia was the birthplace of two great Islamic dynasties: the Seljuqs (571/1075-718/1318), who introduced Islam to the region; and the Ottomans (699/1299-1340/1922), who brought about the end of the Byzantine Empire upon capturing Constantinople, and asserted their hegemony throughout the region.

Selimiye Mosque, general view, Edirne, Turkey.

A distinctive style of Seljuq art and architecture flourished with influences from Central Asia, Iran, Mesopotamia and Syria, which merged with elements deriving from Anatolian Christian and antiquity heritage. Konya, the new capital in Central Anatolia, as well as other cities, were enriched with buildings in the newly developed Seljuq style. Numerous mosques, *madrasa*s, *turbe*s and *caravanserais*, which were richly decorated by stucco and tiling with diverse figural representations, have survived to our day.

Tile of Kubadabad Palace, Karatay Museum, Konya, Turkey.

As the Seljuq Emirates disintegrated and Byzantium declined, the Ottomans expanded their territory swiftly changing their capital from Iznik to Bursa and then again to Edirne. The conquest of Constantinople in 858/1453 by Sultan Mehmet II provided the necessary impetus for the transition of an emerging state into a great empire. A superpower that extended its boundaries to Vienna including the Balkans in the West and to Iran in the East, as well

Great Mosque of Cordoba, mihrab, Spain.

Madinat al-Zahra', Dar al-Yund, Spain.

as North Africa from Egypt to Algeria, turning the Eastern Mediterranean into an Ottoman sea. The race to surpass the grandeur of the inherited Byzantine churches, exemplified by the Hagia Sophia, culminated in the construction of great mosques in Istanbul. The most significant one is the Mosque of Süleymaniye, built in the $10^{th}/16^{th}$ century by the famous Ottoman architect Sinan, it epitomises the climax in architectural harmony in domed buildings. Most major Ottoman mosques were part of a large building complex called *kulliye* that also consisted several *madrasas*, a *Qur'an* school, a library, a hospital (*darussifa*), a hostel (*tabhane*), a public kitchen, a *caravanserai* and mausoleums (*turbes*). From the beginning of the $12^{th}/18^{th}$ century, during the so-called Tulip Period, Ottoman architecture and decorative style reflected the influence of French Baroque and Rococo, heralding the Westernisation period in arts and architecture.

Al-Andalus at the western part of the Islamic world became the cradle of a brilliant artistic and cultural expression. 'Abd al-Rahman I established an independent Umayyad caliphate (138/750-422/1031) with Cordoba as its capital. The Great Mosque of Cordoba would pioneer innovative artistic tendencies such as the double-tiered arches with two alternating colours and panels with vegetal ornamentation which would become part of the repertoire of al-Andalus artistic forms.

In the $5^{th}/11^{th}$ century, the caliphate of Cordoba broke up into a score of principalities incapable of preventing the progressive advance of the reconquest initiated by the Christian states of the Northwestern Iberian Peninsula. These petty kings, or Taifa Kings, summoned the Almoravids in 479/1086 and the Almohads in 540/1145 in order to repel the Christians and re-established partial unity in al-Andalus. Through their intervention in the Iberian Peninsula, the Almoravids (427/1036-541/1147) came into contact with a new civilisations and were captivated quickly by the refinement of al-Andalus art as reflected in their capital, Marrakesh, where they built a grand mosque and palaces. The influence of the architecture of Cordoba and other capitals such as Seville would be felt in all of the Almoravid monuments from Tlemcen, Algiers to Fez.

Tinmal Mosque, aerial view, Morocco.

Under the rule of the Almohads (515/1121-667/1269), who expanded their hegemony as far as Tunisia, Western Islamic art reached its climax. During this period, artistic creativity that originated with the Almoravid rulers was renewed and masterpieces of Islamic art were created. The Great Mosque of Seville with its minaret the Giralda, the Kutubiya in Marrakesh, the Mosque of Hassan in Rabat and the Mosque of Tinmal high in the Atlas Mountains in Morocco are notable examples.

Ladies Tower and Gardens, Alhambra, Granada, Spain.

Upon the dissolution of the Almohad Empire, the Nasrid Dynasty (629/1232-897/1492) installed itself in Granada and was to experience a period of splendour in the $8^{th}/14^{th}$ century. The civilisation of Granada would become a cultural

Mertola, general view, Portugal.

model in future centuries in Spain (Mudejar Art) and particularly in Morocco, where this artistic tradition enjoyed great popularity and would be preserved until the present day in the areas of architecture and decoration, music and cuisine. The famous palace and fort of *al-Hamra'* (the Alhambra) in Granada marks the crowning achievement of al-Andalus art, with all features of its artistic repertoire.

Decoration detail, Abu Inan Madrasa, Meknes, Morocco.

At the same time in Morocco, the Merinids (641/1243-876/1471) replaced the Almohads, while in Algeria the 'Abd al-Wadid's reigned (633/1235-922/1516), as did the Hafsids (625/1228-941/1534) in Tunisia. The Merinids perpetuated al-Andalus art, enriching it with new features. They embellished their capital Fez with an abundance of mosques, palaces and *madrasa*s, with their clay mosaic and *zellij* panelling in the wall decorations, considered

Qal'a of the Bani Hammad, minaret, Algeria.

Sa'adian Tomb Marrakesh, Morocco.

to be the most perfect works of Islamic art. The later Moroccan dynasties, the Sa'adians (933/1527-1070/1659) and the 'Alawite (1077/1659 – until the present day), carried on the artistic tradition of al-Andalus that was exiled from its native soil in 897/1492. They continued to build and decorate their monuments using the same formulas and the same decorative themes as had the preceding dynasties, adding innovative touches characteristic of their creative genius. In the early 11th/17th century, emigrants from al-Andalus (the *Moriscos*), who took up residence in the northern cities of Morocco, introduced numerous features of al-Andalus art. Today, Morocco is one of the few countries that has kept traditions of al-Andalus alive in its architecture and furniture, at the same time modernising them as they incorporated the architectural techniques and styles of the 15th/20th century.

ARCHITECTURAL SUMMARY

In general terms, Islamic architecture can be classified into two categories: religious, such as mosques, *madrasa*s, mausoleums, and secular, such as palaces, *caravanserai*s, fortifications, etc.

Religious Architecture

Mosques

The mosque for obvious reasons lies at the very heart of Islamic architecture. It is an apt symbol of the faith that it serves. That symbolic role was understood by Muslims at a very early stage, and played an important part in the creation of suitable visual markers for the building: minaret, dome, *mihrab*, *minbar*, etc.

The first mosque in Islam was the courtyard of the Prophet's house in Medina, with no architectural refinements. Early mosques built by the Muslims as their empire was expanding were simple. From these buildings developed the congregational or Friday mosque (*jami'*), essential features of which remain today unchanged for nearly 1400 years. The general plan consists of a large courtyard surrounded by arched porticoes, with more aisles or arcades on the side facing Mecca (*qibla*) than the other sides. The Great Umayyad Mosque in Damascus, which followed the plan of the Prophet's Mosque, became the prototype for many mosques built in various parts of the Islamic world.

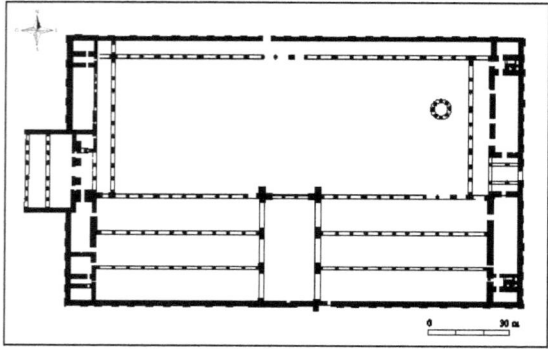

Umayyad Mosque of Damascus, Syria.

Two other types of mosques developed in Anatolia and afterwards in the Ottoman domains: the basilical and the dome types. The first type is a simple pillared hall or basilica that follows late Roman and Byzantine Syrian traditions, introduced with some modifications in the $5^{th}/11^{th}$ century. The second type, which developed during the Ottoman period, has its organisation of interior space under a single dome. The Ottoman architects in great imperial mosques created a new style of domed construction by merging the Islamic mosque tradition with that of dome building in Anatolia. The main dome rests on a hexagonal support system, while lateral bays are covered by smaller domes. This emphasis on an interior space dominated by a single dome became the starting point of a style that was to be introduced in the 10th/16th century. During this period, mosques became multipurpose social com-

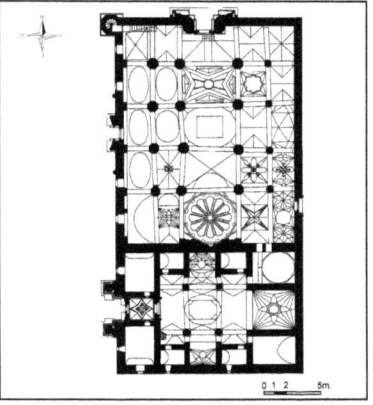

Great Mosque, Divriği, Turkey.

plexes consisting of a *zawiya*, a *madrasa*, a public kitchen, a bath, a *caravanserai* and a mausoleum of the founder. The supreme monument of this style is the Sülaymeniye Mosque in Istanbul built in 965/1557 by the great architect Sinan.

The minaret from the top of which the *muezzin* calls Muslims to prayer, is the most prominent marker of the mosque. In Syria the traditional minaret consists of a square-plan tower built of stone. In Mamluk Egypt minarets are each divided into three distinct zones: a square section at the bottom, an octagonal middle section and a circular section with a small dome on the top. Its shaft is richly decorated and the transition between each section is covered with a band of *muqarnas* decoration. Minarets in North Africa and Spain, that share the square-tower form with Syria, are decorated with panels of motifs around paired sets of windows. During the Ottoman period the octagonal or cylindrical minarets replaced the square tower. Often these are tall pointed minarets and although mosques generally have only one minaret, in major cities there are two, four or even six minarets.

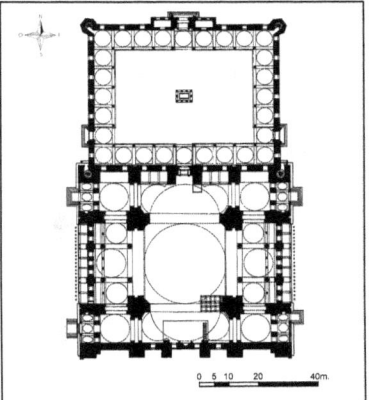

Sülaymeniye Mosque, Istanbul, Turkey.

Typology of minarets.

Madrasas

It seems likely that the Seljuqs built the first *madrasa*s in Persia in the early 5th/11th century when they were small structures with a domed courtyard and two lateral *iwan*s. A later type developed that has an open courtyard with a central *iwan* and which is surrounded by arcades. During the 6th/12th century in Anatolia, the *madrasa* became multifunctional and was intended to serve as a medical school, mental hospital, a hospice with a public kitchen (*imaret*) and a mausoleum. The promotion of *Sunni* (Orthodox) Islam reached a new zenith in Syria and Egypt under the Zengids and the Ayyubids (6th/12th–early 7th/13th centuries). This era witnessed the introduction of the *madrasa* established by a civic or political leader for the advancement of Islamic jurisprudence. The foundation was funded by an endowment in perpetuity (*waqf*), usually the revenues of land or property in the form of an orchard, shops in a market (*suq*), or a bathhouse (*hammam*). The *madrasa* traditionally followed a cruciform plan with a central court surrounded by four *iwan*s. Soon the *madrasa* became a dominant architectural form with mosques adopting a four-*iwan* plan. The *madrasa* gradually lost its sole religious and political function as a propaganda tool and tended to have a broader civic function, serving as a congregational mosque and a mausoleum for the benefactor.

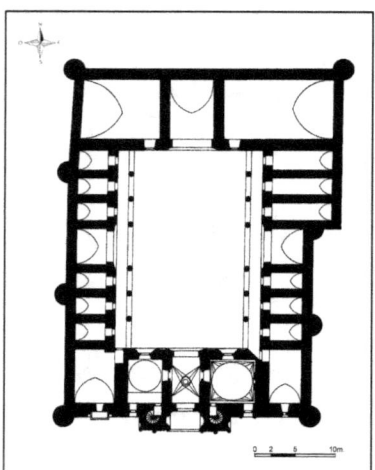

Sivas Gök Madrasa, Turkey.

The construction of *madrasa*s in Egypt, and particularly in Cairo, gathered new momentum with the arrival of the Mamluks. The typical

Cairene *madrasa* of this era was a multifunctional gigantic four-*iwan* structure with a stalactite (*muqarnas*) portal and splendid façades. With the advent of the Ottomans in the 10th/16th century, the joint foundation, typically a mosque-*madrasa*, became a widespread, large complex that enjoyed imperial patronage. The *iwan* disappeared gradually and was replaced by a dominant dome chamber. A substantial increase in the number of domed cells used by students is a characteristic of Ottoman *madrasas*.

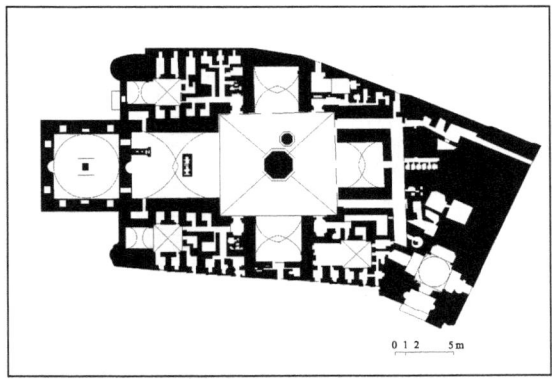

Mosque and Madrasa Sultan Hassan, Cairo, Egypt.

One of the various building types that by virtue of their function and of their form can be related to the *madrasa* is the *khanqa*. The term indicates an institution, rather than a particular kind of building, that houses members of a Muslim mystical (*sufi*) order. Several other words used by Muslim historians as synonyms for *khanqa* include: in the Maghrib, *zawiya*; in Ottoman domain, *tekke*; and in general, *ribat*. *Sufism* permanently dominated the *khanqa*, which originated in eastern Persia during the 4th/10th century. In its simplest form the *khanqa* was a house where a group of pupils gathered around a master (*shaykh*), and it had the facilities for assembly, prayer and communal living. The establishment of *khanqas* flourished under the Seljuqs during the 5th/11th and the 6th/12th centuries and benefited from the close association between *Sufism* and the *Shafi'i madhhab* (doctrine) favoured by the ruling elite.

Mausoleums

The terminology of the building type of the mausoleum used in Islamic sources is varied. The standard descriptive term *turbe* refers to the function of the building as for burial. Another term is *qubba* that refers to the most identifiable, the dome, and often marks a structure commemorating Biblical prophets, companions of the Prophet Muhammad and religious or military notables. The function of mausoleums is not limited simply to a place of burial

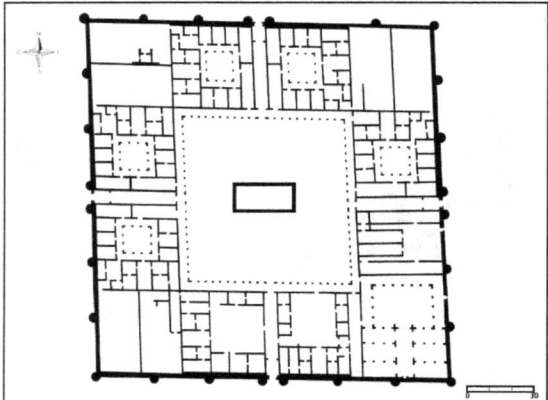

Qasr al-Khayr al-Sharqi, Syria.

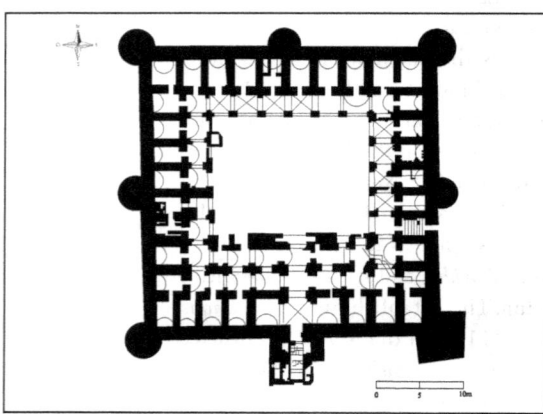

Ribat of Sousse, Tunisia.

and commemoration, but also plays an important role in "popular" religion. They are venerated as tombs of local saints and became places of pilgrimage. Often the structure of a mausoleum is embellished with Qur'anic quotations and contains a *mihrab* within it to render it a place of prayer. In some cases the mausoleum became part of a joint foundation. Forms of medieval Islamic mausoleums are varied, but the traditional one has a domed square plan.

Secular Architecture

Palaces

The Umayyad period is characterised by sumptuous palaces and bathhouses in remote desert regions. Their basic plan is largely derived from Roman military models. Although the decoration of these structures is eclectic, they constitute the best examples of the budding Islamic decorative style. Mosaics, mural paintings, stone or stucco sculpture were used for a remarkable variety of decorations and themes. Abbasid palaces in Iraq, such as those at Samarra and Ukhaidir, follow the same plan as their Umayyad forerunners, but are marked by an increase in size, the use of the great *iwan*, dome and courtyard, and the extensive use of stucco decorations. Palaces in the later Islamic period developed a distinctive style that was more decorative and less monumental. The most remarkable example of royal or princely palaces is the Alhambra. The vast area of the palace is broken up into a series of separate units: gardens, pavilions and courts. The most striking feature of Alhambra, however, is the decoration that provides an extraordinary effect in the interior of the building.

Aksaray Sultan Khan, Turkey.

Caravanserais

A *caravanserai* generally refers to a large structure that provides a lodging place for travellers and merchants. Normally, it has a square or rectangular floor plan, with a single projecting monumental entrance and towers in the exterior walls. A central courtyard is surrounded by porticoes and rooms for lodging travellers, storing merchandise and for the stabling of animals.

The characteristic type of building has a wide range of functions since it has been described as *khan, han, funduq, ribat*. These terms may imply no more than differences in regional vocabularies rather than being distinctive functions or types. The architectural sources of the various types of *caravanserai*s are difficult to identify. Some are perhaps derived from the Roman *castrum* or military camp to which the Umayyad desert palaces are related. Other types, in Mesopotamia and Persia, are associated with domestic architecture.

Urban Organisation

From about the $3^{rd}/10^{th}$ century every town of any significance acquired fortified walls and towers, elaborate gates and a mighty citadel (*qal'a* or *qasba*) as the seat of power. These are massive constructions built in materials characteristic of the region in which they are found; stone in Syria, Palestine and Egypt, or brick, stone and rammed earth in the Iberian Peninsula and North Africa. A unique example of military architecture is the *ribat*. Technically, this is a fortified palace designated for the temporary or permanent warriors of Islam who committed themselves to the defence of frontiers. The *ribat* of Sousse in

Tunisia bears a resemblance to early Islamic palaces, but with a different interior arrangement of large halls, mosque and a minaret.

The division of the majority of Islamic cities into neighbourhoods is based on ethnic and religious affinity and it is also a system of urban organisation that facilitates the administration of the population. In the neighbourhood there is always a mosque. A bathhouse, a fountain, an oven and a group of stores are located either within or nearby. Its structure is formed by a network of streets, alleys and a collection of houses. Depending on the region and era, the home takes on diverse features governed by the historical and cultural traditions, climate and construction materials available.

The market (*suq*), which functions as the nerve-centre for local businesses, would be the most relevant characteristic of Islamic cities. Its distance from the mosque determines the spatial organisation of the markets by specialised guilds. For instance, the professions considered clean and honourable (bookmakers, perfume makers, tailors) are located in the mosque's immediate environs, and the noisy and foul-smelling crafts (blacksmiths, tanning, cloth dying) are situated progressively further from it. This geographic distribution responds to imperatives that rank on strictly technical grounds.

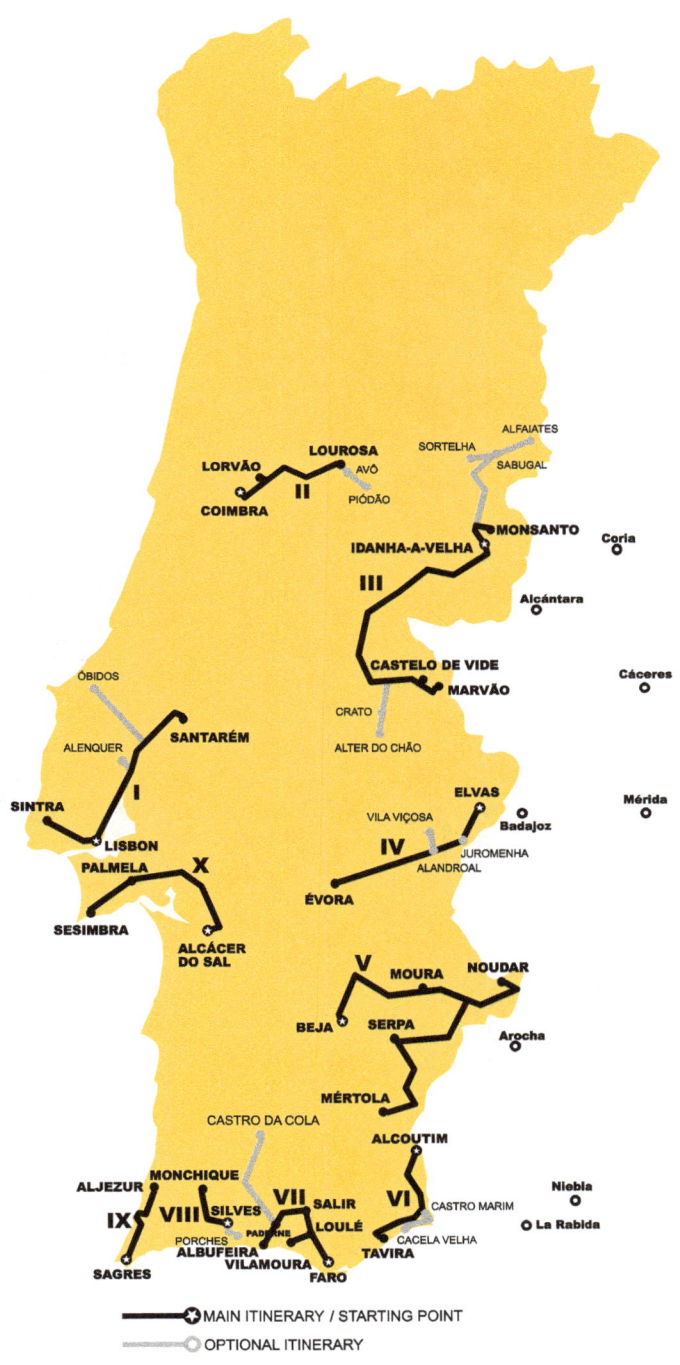

Commemorative tablet for the construction of the mosque's minaret, detail, 444/1052, Moura.

GHARB AL-ANDALUS: A BRIEF HISTORY

Santiago Macias

In chronological terms, the westernmost territories of the Peninsula closely accompanied the Islamicisation process that took place in the other regions of Spain. According to written records, between 95/714 and 97/716, cities such as Lisbon, Faro, Beja, Santarém and Coimbra gradually succumbed to Muslim influence, it being supposed that all of the rest of the territory had been subjected to an identical situation.

The strategy adopted by the first Muslim troops for the occupation of this territory was based mainly on consensus and the drafting of agreements with the Iberian peoples. This fact was to make a decisive contribution towards maintaining a relatively autonomous state in the Gharb that sometimes came very close to achieving almost complete independence.

Seen from the viewpoint of the political history of Islamic civilisation in the Iberian Peninsula, the territory of Gharb al-Andalus represents a unique region, which is characterised by its own particular way of dealing with events taking place in its large centres of decision making. Although the region was somewhat geographically removed from Cordoba and Seville, which encouraged a gradual centralisation of political power between the $2^{nd}/8^{th}$ and $7^{th}/13^{th}$ centuries, certain events took place there that had a decisive effect locally and which were sometimes extremely important for the development of the political history of the Iberian Peninsula as a whole.

Besides the inherent social contradictions between the urban and rural worlds, there was also a widening ethnic, linguistic and even religious gap between the city and the country throughout al-Andalus, and therefore, obviously, in the Gharb itself. This gap grew ever wider with the successive migrations of traders or professional soldiers.

The scattered nature of small and medium-sized cities throughout the territory reveals the dilution of power that, to a certain extent, defined and individualised Gharb al-Andalus in the Iberian context. In this sense, it is symptomatic that Lisbon, the largest and most powerful urban centre in the Gharb, never enjoyed hegemony over the region, nor showed any wish to do so. The Estuary City always played a discreet role throughout the power struggles that systematically involved its neighbours, although it too resisted the control of Cordoba. It should also be remembered that this same city had tried to take over the political inheritance of the former Lusitanian capital and that both attempts made by Badajoz to unify the region were destined to enjoy only short-term success, due to the permanent state of rebellion in the area.

As part of a tradition that seems to have been fairly widespread across the whole of al-Andalus, each city's *caide* or *alcaide* was both the representative and sanctioner of a political and religious power that

Bowl with hunting scenes, $5^{th}/11^{th}$ century, Mértola Museum.

Capital and impost, 7th / 13th century, Mértola Museum.

Marble Capital, 4th / 10th century, National Archaeology Museum, Lisbon.

had to be confirmed through a weekly invocation at the mosque. This fact had little to do with the power effectively wielded by this higher functionary, whose main role was to collect taxes. As was frequently the case in the Gharb, and despite their being accepted by the *caliph* who negotiated a division of power with them, these *alcaide*s were usually local potentates belonging to powerful family groups that already effectively held economic power in the city and region. On two exceptional occasions, the *alcaide*s even took control of the city into their own hands: once with the small fishermen's republic of Pechina, close to Almeria and then, again, in the Gharb, with the maritime commune of Tavira from 545/1151 to 562/1167. This effective exercise of power was in the hands of the rich traders, who assumed their regional origins so completely that they adopted the names of their own cities. The old Roman city of Ossonoba, which took the name of Santa Maria in the 5th/11th century, began to be called Santa Maria de Faro, due to the fact that a lighthouse (*farol*) may have been built there around this time, made necessary by the silting-up of the river delta. The name Faro, therefore, may not derive from an Arabic anthroponym, as is generally stated, but rather the other way round, i.e. that an important local family adopted the name of the city that it had governed for several decades. It was common amongst the *muladi*s – the converts to Islam – to incorporate the name of their birthplace in their Qur'anic name at the same time as they embraced their new faith.

Successive attempts by the emirs and *caliph*s to centralise power frequently came into conflict with the local desire for autonomy, a feeling which was particularly evident amongst the *muladi*s and *Mozarab*s and which did not dwindle over the centuries. In turn, these local rebellions tended to give rise to unifying movements at a regional level. Gharb al-Andalus was to see a series of such initiatives occurring in its territory.

In 145/763, various revolts broke out, supposedly originating in the Yahsubi family. The attitude of the Yahsubis reveals a genuine desire for autonomy in Gharb al-Andalus in that Abd al-Rahman had been obliged to respect the power of this tribe in the south of the Gharb in exchange for recognition of his own authority, with the result that the clan obtained a guarantee of power over the region that it controlled. This revolt had as its mentor the Yahsubi chief al-Ala Ibn Mughit, who proclaimed the sovereignty of the Abbasid *caliph* (the head of the dynasty that reigned in Baghdad), whose representative he considered himself to be in al-Andalus. The rebellion spread from Beja (its point of origin) throughout the Gharb, and was later crushed with some difficulty and only through recourse to betrayal by the Emir Abd al-Rahman I, who sought the help of non-Yemeni Arab leaders. This rebellion was followed by the Revolt of 148/765–66, led by Sa'id al-Yahsubi al-Mattari, and that of 156/773–157/774, led by Abd al-Ghafir al-Yahsubi. Both rebellions seem to clearly express the power of a particularly important tribe in the fight against the central power based in Cordoba.

The main period of *muladi* revolts in the Gharb takes place in the middle of the 3rd/s. h. 9th century, which is also closely connected to the actions of a military leader of great importance in the history of the western region of the Iberian Peninsula: Abd al-Rahman Ibn Marwan al-Jilliqi, the son of the governor with the same name.

Following the first attempted revolt in 254/868, al-Jilliqi (the Galician) was taken to the court of Cordoba, from where he escaped a few years later. He then joined forces with another *muladi*, Sadun Fath al-Surunbaqi, with whom he fought against the Umayyad army.

After a series of military actions, they retreated into Christian territory and Alfonso III of León entrusted al-Surunbaqi with the task of protecting a fortress by the River Douro, while also taking part in various acts of pillage in the south of the Peninsula.

The decidedly ambiguous role played by al-Jilliqi and al-Surunbaqi, who were one moment resident at the emir's court and the next in the service of Christian princes, seems to be rooted precisely in the key position that the whole region of the North Alentejo, and the centre of Portugal, occupied in the context of the Gharb. The successive alliances put into practice by these *muladi* military leaders were no more than a way of asserting the political power of a territory which stretched from Badajoz to the River Douro, and of thereby guaranteeing its autonomy.

The death of Ibn Marwan, which probably occurred in 276/889–890 did not quench this strong thirst for autonomy that had been felt in the Gharb for many decades. The Gharb region remained outside the direct influence of the Emirs of Cordoba for a further 40 years after this. Abd al-Rahman Ibn Marwan established himself in Badajoz and Mérida, whilst Abd al-Malik Ibn Abi al-Jawad took possession of Beja, extending his control as

Marble Tombstone, $4^{th}/10^{th}$ century, IPPAR, Évora.

far as Mértola, whose fortress he restored. Further south, Bakr Ibn Yahya Ibn Bakr, the son of Zadulfo, took charge of Santa Maria. According to the report *Bayan al-Mughrib* "the three of them met to withstand their enemies". This statement provides evidence that solidarity was firmly maintained between the military leaders of the Gharb, as a way of ensuring the continuation of its status, a position that had been won with great difficulty.

The unification achieved by Abd al-Rahman III brought an end to a century-long struggle for the control of Gharb territory. After the Yahsubis had tried to achieve supremacy, and following a long period of domination by the Banu Marwan family over the western region of the Iberian Peninsula, the *caliph* managed to neutralise regional differences for some time and to exercise power over a territory that had always shown itself to be particularly wary of any form of external domination. The various divisions witnessed in Gharb territory throughout the $5^{th}/11^{th}$ century do not only represent an expression of the interests of different Arab tribes or the military leaders' thirst for power, as has so often been suggested. Instead, they signify the systematic and cyclical outbreak of local and regional autonomies. In turn, each outbreak was skilfully manoeuvred by the military and political elite of these regions in order to build a solid base of support for the secessionist temptations of the *cadis* and *walis* who had been placed in front of the *coras* and cities by the authorities in Cordoba. The successive violent rebellions that occurred throughout the Gharb in opposition to central power seems to have enjoyed immediate enthusiastic support of the people in the region.

In the district of Ossonoba the importance of the *muladi* and *Mozarab* communities was quite considerable. At the level of toponymy, in addition to the name of the city itself ("Santa Maria" – a name which curiously was only re-adopted in the Islamic period), there was also mention of a settlement known as Sanbras (São Brás de Alportel?), that was the birthplace of the poet Ibn Ammar. Furthermore, the importance of several Christian places of worship gives us an idea of the influence of the Christians in the southern regions of al-Andalus. In addition to the existence of a church in Sagres, it was also said that the silver columns of the Church of Santa Maria were so wide that one man alone could not embrace them. Although this is a rather fanciful statement it provides evidence of the importance the Christian community had in the context of the city and certainly in the context of the region. As local leaders, the Banu Harun, whether or not they were *muladi*s, took responsibility in representing the interests of that vast community.

One last attempt at regional unification was made under the inspiration of the religious leader Ibn Qasi, who during the period of the second *Taifa* kingdoms (in the mid-$6^{th}/12^{th}$ century) succeeded in forcing the districts of Mértola, Silves, Beja and Évora into submitting to his rule. The weakening of Almoravid power in the Gharb resulted in the appearance of the second *Taifa* kingdoms in the region. Now religious motivation disguised clearly defined political interests which developed concurrently with the Christian onslaught of 533/1139 to 541/1147, causing the borders of the emerging kingdom of Portugal to advance as far as the line of the River Tagus. It was during these campaigns that two crucial cities,

Santarém and Lisbon, were captured from the sphere of Islamic influence.

The leader of the Gharb rebellion was Abu al-Qasim al-Husayn Ibn Qasi, a *muladi*, originating from an important family in Silves, who had devoted his youth to the study of Muslim theologians and who began to preach a life of asceticism. He even ordered a hermitage to be built in the district of Silves, to which he withdrew with his group of disciples, known as *Muridins* (novices). The volatile political atmosphere that prevailed in the Gharb at this time proved to be propitious for the implantation of the ambitious intentions of Ibn Qasi, who engaged in important political and military activity throughout this region from 538/1144 onwards.

It was in fact one of his followers who took the Castle of Mértola in 538/1144, the place where Ibn Qasi was to make a triumphant entrance some days later. Ibn Qasi's rise to power once again led to the Gharb becoming an autonomous political body: the rebellions of Abu Muhammad Sidray Ibn Wazir in Beja, and Abu Walid Muhammad Ibn al-Mundir in Silves, took place immediately afterwards and clearly confirmed this trend, which was further strengthened by their subsequent surrender to Ibn Qasi. Next, al-Mundir conquered Huelva and Niebla, whilst Ibn Wazir expanded these dominions as far as Badajoz.

Having been deposed, Ibn Qasi travelled to Africa to seek the help of the Almohads, who gave him command of the City of Silves in 541/1147. The reign of Ibn Qasi came to an end very shortly after, however, when the pact that he established with D. Afonso Henriques led to his assassination in Silves in 545/1151. The last 100 years of Islamicisation were marked by a series of military campaigns led by the lords from the North. The beginning of these campaigns can be situated a little before the mid-$6^{th}/12^{th}$ century, with the conquest of two cities that were fundamental to the control of the boundary established by the River Tagus: Santarém and Lisbon, which were taken in 540/1146–541/1147.

The second half of the $6^{th}/12^{th}$ century was marked both by the influence that the Almohads exerted over the south of the Iberian Peninsula and by a period during which the Christian military campaigns became more resolute and more devastating. Between 560/1165 and 567/1172, the new Portuguese kingdom included the northernmost territories of the Alentejo, an area that corresponded, roughly speaking, with the district of Évora. Shortly afterwards, in 579/1184, there was a significant attack led by Abu Ya'qub Yusuf, who in his attempt to re-conquer Santarém was wounded and died before reaching Évora.

Leaving aside the raids carried out by D. Sancho I in 584/1189, and those led by Ya'qub al-Mansur in subsequent years, it is evident that the most decisive events were those that took place between 613/1217 and 647/1250. It was these events that culminated in the conquest of what remained of the Alentejo and subsequently the whole of the Algarve.

THE FAR WEST OF IBERIA

Cláudio Torres

Besides being the source of the world's oldest maritime and urban civilisations, the geoclimatic frontiers of the Mediterranean mark the territorial boundaries and spaces into which the Roman Empire initially, and subsequently Islam, were to become firmly implanted. Islamic civilisation cannot be divorced from its geographical and cultural context. We cannot explain the religious changes that took place in the 1st/7th century, coupled with the remarkable Muslim expansion, by mentioning only the invasions of peoples originating from Arabia and other desert strips on the fringes of the civilised world of the great maritime cities. Islamicisation is a complex process that cannot be dissociated from the traditions of Mediterranean urban life, where religious systems, and Christianity in particular, were being torn apart at that time by serious theological schisms. The new religious mysticism, the search for one's origins, the good news of the *Qur'an*, all this was assimilated and disseminated in this urban merchant environment and certainly not imposed at the edge of a sword by military squadrons of professional warmongers.

If we accept these premises, then we shall be better able to understand the social political and artistic phenomena nurtured during the centuries of Iberian Islam which defined a civilisation with an unrepeatable and peculiar style all of its own. The history of the Iberian Peninsula has been marked, traditionally, by the invasion of the army led by Tarik in 92/711 and by the mythical battle of Guadalete, when the Christian forces were defeated by the Saracens and forced to seek refuge in the mountains to the north. Today, however, in order to explain such a rapid and efficient process of religious conversion, which spread quickly throughout almost the whole of the Iberian Peninsula, contemporary archaeological research and, generally speaking, more recent historiography, have tended to devalue the military facts (namely by converting many demobilised soldiers into settlers). In this way they have highlighted instead a process of contamination and cultural synthesis led by sailors, merchants and muleteers, who took advantage of the opening up of the great maritime routes and the development of cities.

Instead of scenarios involving urban destruction and ruined buildings, instead of scars being left by the imposition of new forms of civilisation, what is in fact notable from the 3rd/9th century onwards is a widespread resurgence of cities. There was an intensification of the already perceptible move towards the architectural and decorative fashions of the old Byzantine Empire of the East — where Damascus had established itself as the capital — and Proconsular Africa (present-day

Bowl with hunting scenery 5th/11th century, Mértola Museum.

Tunisia). In fact, at least as far as the Iberian Peninsula is concerned (and this is confirmed in particular by archaeological information), the first complete civilisational transformation (already clearly visible in the earlier sequence of Mediterranean events) did not in fact occur during the end of 1st/early 8th century. What traditional history refers to as the great Hagarene invasions are in fact the years of the "Reconquest", when the first "foreign bodies" were introduced into the south of the peninsula, bringing with them a new form of social organisation that can generally be categorised as feudalism.

Rather than being imposed by military means, the Islamicisation of the Iberian Peninsula resulted from a rapid conversion of the urban populations, more than anything, who were more open to the exchange of merchandise and ideas. The opening of new routes and markets was naturally accompanied and encouraged by an evident increase in the quantity and variety of products and artefacts. In addition to creating new tastes and appetites, the imports of cloth, ceramics, weapons and wrought metals (sometimes from far-off lands) stimulated local manufacturers, which, whilst preserving some references to their original models, soon acquired autonomy, thereby initiating innovative aesthetic languages and consolidating other regional trade circuits. Despite frequent commercial relations between the Eastern Mediterranean and al-Andalus – referred to in certain well-known $5^{th}/11^{th}$ century documents housed at the Genisa synagogue in Cairo – one of the largest supply centres for the markets of the Gharb seems to have been the region of Tunis and Kairouan (in present-day Tunisia). These two cities recovered their importance as cultural and religious cen-

Marble Capital, $4^{th}/10^{th}$ century, National Archaeology Museum, Lisbon.

tres during the $3^{rd}/9^{th}$ and $4^{th}/10^{th}$ centuries. In the Western Mediterranean, economic interchanges and cultural bonds were just as intense during this period as they had been during the times of Saint Augustine (5th century). At this time, the architectural and decorative models of Christian art of old Carthage had served as the model for the basilicas and baptisteries of southern Hispania.

Only after the $4^{th}/10^{th}$ and $5^{th}/11^{th}$ centuries did the coastal strip of Western Algeria and the modern-day ports of Ceuta and Tangier begin to develop under the influence of Cordoba and the other capitals in al-Andalus, which had unquestionably established itself as the main attraction throughout the region. Crossing the Gulf of the Algarve, or the Sea of Alboran, and connecting Faro to Asilah or Almeria to Algeria, became much easier and quicker than, say, travelling between Tavira and Lisbon, a route that was exposed to the rough seas and adverse winds off the Cape of St. Vincent. In the west of the Iberian Peninsula, Gharb al-Andalus presented itself as the natural heir of the former Lusitania. Its frontiers with the territories of Cordoba and Seville coincided with the extremities of the Roman province of Baetica.

*Marble Capital,
3rd/9th-4th/10th
century, Municipal
Museum Pedro Nunes,
Alcácer do Sal.*

*Marble Capital,
4th/10th century,
National Archaeology
Museum, Lisbon.*

One of the most innovative phenomena in the Islamicisation of the Gharb is to be noted in the role played by the native populations, who were Islamicised over a period of more than five centuries. Up to the mid-5th/10th century, most of the people living in this far-western end of the Iberian Peninsula were still non-Muslim. A process of Arabisation was rapidly instituted, however, which leads us to think that the part played by the *Mozarab*s in this context was certainly much greater than was in fact generally recognised but a short while ago. In adapting to the new order that, after all, favoured decentralised urban powers, the old Visigothic church was pulverised into a few bishoprics that continued for many years afterwards to act as the representatives of the *Mozarab* communities in their not-always hostile dialogue with the *alcaide*s and Muslim authorities.

Although a certain amount of destructive anger may have followed the occupation of the territories further to the south and, later on, the rigours of the Counter-Reformation may have erased many other traces of the process of Islamicisation, the complete extinction of Arabised or Mediterranean Portugal has always met with strong resistance and, fortunately, never been fully achieved.

In this territory, which was later integrated into the kingdom of Portugal, there is not an abundance of large courtly or military monuments from the Islamic period. In fact, the material remains and artefacts from this time currently in museums really amount to very few. Although the lack of ancient material remains places the region on the fringes of the great centres of Andalusian civilisation, it also leads us to believe that its distance from the influences of Cordoba and the clear incorporation of native motifs, served to reinforce a certain regional singularity.

As is natural, these particularities are not to be seen in religious or palatine building programmes, where the same language and decorative features continue to be found albeit at a provincial scale. Instead, it is in the size and volume of the structures, the building techniques and the functional or decorative complements of popular architecture that the memory of the Andalusian symbiosis has remained most clearly visible. Without this, it would be impossible to explain the 16th-century explosion in *Mudejar* decoration, *Manueline* art and the creative Alentejo Gothic style, in which bold vaulting techniques and delicate mouldings blend together harmoniously with the knowledgeable use of polychrome glazed tile coverings.

Perhaps the most subtle influences of the Moors (who continue to inhabit the dream-filled nights of popular romances) are to be found rooted in the sorrowful sounds of Alentejo choirs, the subtly patterned braiding found amongst Coimbra weavers, the virtuous painted rims of Redondo ceramic plates and in the aromas and flavours of an Algarvian *escabeche* (vinegar sauce).

In pointing out and opening up some of the old southern routes, this brief guide to the lands of the Enchanted Moorish Maiden seeks to highlight the profusion of small marks that, after all, intertwine and define Mediterranean Portugal and the very raison d'être of Islamic civilisation.

Certain popular traditions are still very much alive today. The moss-covered stones of a castle, the proud ruins of a bridge, a giant rock from which there springs a stream of crystal-clear water, all that is mysterious and inexplicable comes from the time of the Moors or is under the spell of an enchanted Moorish Maiden.

Since the Moors were defeated, an oft-repeated legend has always maintained that, on certain moonlit nights, whoever dares to wander through the Serra de Sintra or the dark woods of Buçaco will see an extremely beautiful maiden dressed in white emerge from an opening next to a rock. The young girl in white, with a water-pot by her side, can be seen hurrying to a spring of cool water. As she passes by with the pot on her head, there echoes in the silence the restrained but doleful moaning of a time that will never again return.

Tombstone with epigram, Faro Archaeological Museum.

ITINERARY I

Mudejar Art

Cláudio Torres, Santiago Macias, Maria Regina Anacleto,
Ruben de Carvalho, Cristina Garcia, Paula Noronha

I.1 LISBON
    I.1.a City Museum
    I.1.b National Archaeology
          Museum
    I.1.c Cathedral
    I.1.d St. George's Castle
    I.1.e The Moorish Wall
    I.1.f Alfama Quarter

Fado

I.2 SINTRA
    I.2.a Vila Palace
    I.2.b Pena Palace
    I.2.c The Moorish Castle
    I.2.d Monserrate Palace and
          Gardens

I.3 ALENQUER (option)
    I.3.a Islamic Alenquer

I.4 ÓBIDOS (option)
    I.4.a Historical town of Óbidos

I.5 SANTARÉM
    I.5.a Santarém Municipal Museum
          - São João de Alporão

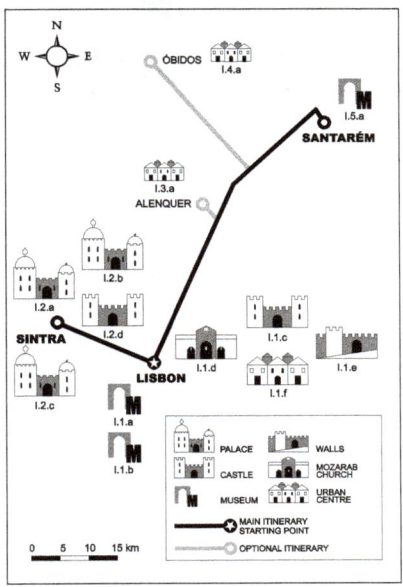

*Pena Palace,
detail, Sintra.*

45

ITINERARY I   *Mudejar Art*

The Moorish Castle, Sintra.

The vast estuary of the River Tagus formed an inland sea that was prolonged by a dense network of canals, navigable as far as Abrantes, Coruche or Tomar. Here was the origin of a settlement capable of allying the most advanced arts of fishing and the cultivation of the fertile mud flats of the Ribatejo to the most careful tendering of orchards and vegetable gardens. For many centuries the various harbours in this inland-sea (popularly known as the Mar da Palha or Sea of Straw) were the westernmost points of the Mediterranean routes, making it possible to successfully blend together shipbuilding techniques with naval experience. Then, at the end of the period of Islamic civilisation, sea routes were opened up across the Bay of Biscay and the northern seas.

The Christian Conquest of the mid-$6^{th}/12^{th}$ century does not seem to have affected the riverside populations of fishermen and sailors, who, just like the local country folk (known as saloios), continued to leave the marks of their own particular civilisation upon this region. The reasons for this are undoubtedly related to the region's density of population. Lisbon and its surrounding areas benefited from the activities of the Moorish community until the end of the 15th century. Besides leaving its stamp on the region's place names and the people's careful ten-

ITINERARY I   Mudejar Art
Lisbon

dering of their vegetable patches and gardens, the Mudejar way of life influenced the architectural fashions of the palatine arts of the 16th century Manueline style and even the Romantic revivalism that was to follow on much later.

C. T.

1.1 LISBON

At the end of the 6th/12th century, Lisbon was clearly already the largest urban centre in Gharb al-Andalus. If we add the 15 hectares of space inside the city walls to the two residential quarters of Alfama and west Lisbon beyond the walls, its urban area amounted to approximately 30 hectares. Taking into account the dense settlement throughout the suburbs and along the riverbank, it is quite likely that there was a population of some 20-25,000 inhabitants concentrated in this area.

As was the case in other similar city-ports, two main centres can be clearly identified around which the population grew. At the highest point of the hill there stood the citadel, a residential palace for an elite of courtiers; by the riverside, there was a profuse accumulation of fishermen, artisans and traders, who together formed the lower city. Their merging together into one large body was already confirmed by the end of the 4th-b. 5th/b. 11th century. The palace where the *alcaide* or governor resided was on the hilltop (the present-day residential quarter of Santa Cruz) together with other residences of the palace officers.

Leaving the *medina* by the western side, in the area close to the main mosque, one would have entered another urban labyrinth spreading sharply down the hillside to an inlet from the sea, which served as the city's harbour. On its sandy beaches, carpenters and caulkers could be seen building and repairing boats.

One of the Muslim cemeteries spread out eastwards, on the site where the Monastery of São Vicente was built after the Christian conquest, undoubtedly flank-

St. George's Castle, Lisbon.

ITINERARY I   *Mudejar Art*
Lisbon

City Museum, Lisbon.

ing and overlapping with other ancient Palaeo-Christian burial grounds. Also in the eastern part of the city, but closer to the river, were the shops of the gold- and silversmiths and the silk and brocade merchants. These were the *qaysariyya*, where customs duties were also charged.

C. T.

I.1.a City Museum

Campo Grande, 245, tel: 21 757 17 25/6/7. Entrance fee. Open: 10.00-13.00 and 14.00-18.00. Closed on Mondays and public holidays.

The building which houses the City Museum is a remarkable mid-18th-century construction, which has been a listed building since 1936, although neither its commissioner nor architect are known. It is currently known as the Palácio Pimenta (the name of one of its former owners) and was purchased by the Lisbon City Council in 1962. Today, the museum houses a permanent exhibition about the city's history, organised into chronological and thematic groups.

Although the collection from the Islamic period is considered to be relatively unimportant, attention is drawn to a plaque showing the chronology of emirates ($3^{rd}/9^{th}$-$4^{th}/10^{th}$ centuries) and two tombstones written in Arabic.

Plaque

Although for many years it was classified as Visigothic, it is now accepted that this plaque (found in Rua dos Bacalhoeiros) dates from a later period. The parallels that it reveals with near-eastern art, and in particular with features that have been identified in Khirbat al-Mafjar in Palestine, have led the art historian Manuel Real to review its date and to include it amongst the productions of a Lisbon workshop that was particularly active during this period.

Tombstone N.º 1

After the city's Reconquest, this tombstone belonged to Mouraria (the Moorish Quarter) and was found in Praça da

ITINERARY I   *Mudejar Art*
Lisbon

Figueira in 1962, during excavation work for the Lisbon underground railway. It is a curious piece dating from the end of the 14th century (the most recent one of its kind in Portugal) and has the following words inscribed upon it: "In the name of God, the Clement, the Merciful. God blesses Muhammad and his family. This is the tomb of al-Abbas Ahmad Ibn [... died] on the first Monday of Shawwal in the year 800 of the Hegira. May God have compassion upon him".

Tombstone, 800/1398, City Museum, Lisbon.

Tombstone, 6th/12th-7th/13th century, City Museum, Lisbon.

Tombstone N.º 2

Found in Rua das Madres (Madragoa Quarter), this tombstone bears certain similarities to the tombstone of Frielas belonging to the National Archaeology Museum. It must date from a fairly late period (6th/end of the 12th century or even from the 7th/13th century) and has the following Qur'anic inscription: "All that is found upon the Earth shall disappear. Only the face of thy Lord will remain adorned with majesty and nobility".

S. M.

I.1.b National Archaeology Museum

Praça do Império, tel: 21 362 00 00. Entrance fee. Open: 10.00-18.00. Closed on Mondays and 1st January, Easter, 1st May and 25th December.

Since the end of the 19th century, the National Archaeology Museum has occupied part of the western wing of the Mosteiro dos Jerónimos, a building that was classified as a National Monument in 1907. Until roughly 20 years ago, the museum exhibited a permanent collection of archaeological and ethnographic material, in which there was a place for a small sample of the so-called "Portuguese-Arab" pieces. The permanent

ITINERARY I   Mudejar Art
Lisbon

National Archaeology Museum, Lisbon.

Tombstone of Frielas, e. $6^{th}/12^{th}$–b. $7^{th}/13^{th}$ century, National Archaeology Museum, Lisbon.

exhibition inaugurated in 1989 excluded this sector and the examples of the city's Islamic past were sent to the museum's reserve collection. The cycle of temporary exhibitions that began in 1994 culminated in the opening of the exhibition entitled "Islamic Portugal. The last signs of the Mediterranean" in 1998.

In João Saavedra Machado's work about the history of the Museum (known at that time as the Dr. Leite de Vasconcelos Ethnological Museum) and published in 1964, the only reference made to the museum's Islamic treasures amount to the following text: "The Ethnological Museum has only a few objects from this period: sculptures (decorated capitals and column bases), decorated friezes, a font, tombstones with inscriptions, ceramics and bronze artefacts".

Since then, a few objects from the Islamic period have been incorporated into a collection that was basically the one inherited from the time of Leite de Vasconcelos, the greatest Portuguese ethnologist of the first half of the 20th century. Although small, this collection includes pieces of undeniable quality, amongst which is the tombstone found at Frielas (Loures), the Cacela ablutions font and two capitals from the time of the *caliph*s.

Tombstone

The upper part of an epitaph does not have a date and bears no reference to the deceased person. It dates from the end of $6^{th}/12^{th}$-$7^{th}/13^{th}$ century. The arch that frames the inscription continued to be commonly used in the Lisbon region, as can be seen from the tombstones at the City Museum.

ITINERARY I *Mudejar Art*
Lisbon

The inscription on the stone reads: "God is eternal. Have compassion according to thy mercy, oh Thou who ruleth over all, and look [with mercy] upon the place whither I am sent [...]".

Ablutions Font

This font can be dated to the second half of 6th/12th century and belonged to the collection of the archaeologist Estácio da Veiga. Circular in shape, with eight lobes, this rare piece would have been used for performing ritual ablutions. The letters, which are bare-

Cacela's Ablutions Font, s. h. 6th/12th century, National Archaeology Museum, Lisbon.

Cathedral, excavations in the cloister, Lisbon.

ITINERARY I   *Mudejar Art*
Lisbon

St. George's Castle, Lisbon.

ly distinguishable, would have been part of a quotation from the *Qur'an*.

S. M.

I.1.c **Cathedral**

Largo da Sé, tel: 21 886 67 52.
Entrance fee to cloister. Open: 9.00-17.00 daily.

Close to the city's Porta Férrea (Iron Gate) there once stood the main Lisbon Mosque, on the site where the cathedral now stands. Building work began on the latter church in 539/1145, after the city's conquest by the Christians. According to contemporary descriptions, the mosque had seven naves and – in view of the architectural features that were later re-used – seems to have been an adaptation of an earlier basilica.

Recent archaeological excavations carried out inside the cathedral's Gothic cloister have unearthed several stages in the historical occupation of Lisbon and also an annex – possibly a washroom – of the mosque. Here, a store of silver coins minted in the end of 5th-b. 6th/f. h. 12th century was found hidden inside part of the plumbing system. These are now kept at the National Archaeology Museum.

C. T.

I.1.d **St. George's Castle**

Rua do Chão da Feira.
Open: 9.00-20.00 daily.

In the mid-$6^{th}/12^{th}$ century, in a letter addressed to Osberno, it was stated: "To the north of the river is the city of Lisbon,

ITINERARY I *Mudejar Art*
Lisbon

standing atop a rounded hill, whose fortifications, descending in flights, come down to the banks of the Tagus, being separated from this only by the wall".
The Islamic citadel, with its own fortifications, occupied an area of four hectares on the top of this hill. In addition to the governor's palace and the buildings used by his court, the rest of the area, which now forms the residential quarter of Santa Cruz, would have been occupied by the houses of the government officials and soldiers.
After centuries of successive reoccupations, restoration work, earthquakes and frequent neglect, little has remained visible of the old Islamic fortification at St. George's Castle. There are a few remains of the citadel, but most of these were erased during the 15th and 16th centuries, when major rebuilding work was undertaken and the general structure of the castle was adapted to form royal palaces and reshaped to the taste of successive Portuguese kings and queens. For this reason, almost all of the decorative features to be found dotted about the castle precinct belong to 16th-century architectural models.
In the north-facing area of the castle (close to the Church of Menino de Deus), there still remains a short section and turret of the original Islamic wall, dating from the 5th/11th century.

S. M. / C. T.

Follow Rua do Chão da Feira and continue along Travessa do Funil. Then continue through Largo do Contador-Mor, turn left and follow the tramlines to Largo de Santa Luzia.

I.1.e **The Moorish Wall**

Section of wall close to the Igreja do Menino de Deus in Calçada do Menino de Deus.

Inside an enormous wall built around the whole city in the 14th century, it is still possible to see the old Moorish wall that joined the citadel to the riverside quarters at the end of 4th-b. 5th/b. 11th century.
This marriage of the two areas into one single body was confirmed by the building of a solid stone wall with, quadrangular towers, which was 2 km. thick.
The citadel, which had its own defensive system, occupied an area of four hectares on the top of the hill. On the western side, the exit from the *medina* was through the monumental Porta Férrea (Iron Gate). Beside the western suburbs, but further north, was the Porta da Alfofa (Wicket Gate). The Porta do Mar (Sea Gate) stood facing the beach.

The Moorish Wall, Lisbon.

ITINERARY I *Mudejar Art*
Lisbon

Street in Alfama, Lisbon.

On the eastern side was the so-called Porta do Sol (Sun Gate) or cemetery gate and, closer to the river, a large barbican protected the Porta da Alfama (Alfama Gate). A number of original sections from this imposing walled fortification can still be seen, notably the east-facing walls and turrets of the citadel close to the Igreja do Menino de Deus and the base of the Capela de Santa Luzia.

C. T.

Walk down Calçada do Menino de Deus and follow the tramline to Largo das Portas do Sol.

I.1.f **Alfama Quarter**

From Largo das Portas do Sol, walk down Rua Rosa Araújo, turn right and continue along Rua de São Miguel. Turn left into Beco do Mexias and left again along Rua de São Pedro, passing through Largo do Chafariz de Dentro, until you reach Chafariz d'el Rey.

The houses of Alfama tumble down to the river in a tangled labyrinth of narrow streets and steps. This residential quarter, where the Mediterranean tradition of cramped *medina*s was once again imposed, is today one of the most typical districts of Lisbon and undeniably the one that affords the city its most profound sense of history and character. Its name derives from the Arabic term for thermal springs: *al-hama*. In fact, hot-spring waters can still be found here and until quite recently were used by the local women to wash their clothes. In Islamic times, this was a residential quarter inhabited by fishermen and artisans and stood outside the walls of the city, with which it communicated through the gate known as the Porta da Alfama.

C. T.

FADO

Ruben de Carvalho

Casa do Fado e da Guitarra Portuguesa.
Largo do Chafariz de Dentro, 1, Alfama, tel:
21 882 34 70.
Open: spring/summer: 10.00-18.00; autumn/winter: 10.00 -17.00
Closed: Tuesday and 1st January, 1st May and 25th December.

Cascading down the hillside from St. George's Castle are the residential quarters of Alfama and Mouraria, the oldest areas of Lisbon and a part of the urban fabric that most successfully withstood the destruction wreaked by the earthquake in 1755. Alfama had served, since Roman times, as the connection between the fortress and the river, whilst Mouraria opened onto the countryside to the north and west. The Arab presence in these two quarters can still be seen in their actual names, which have been preserved until the present day and continue to reveal the multicultural flavour that this area has always enjoyed, welcoming into its midst Christian, Muslim and Jewish populations. This multicultural aspect was further enhanced by the importance of the Port of Lisbon, especially from the 15th century onwards. Not only was there much coming and going of different crews, but there was also a sizeable black population of slaves and freedmen from Africa and Brazil, who came to settle in the area, particularly in Alfama.

This intermingling of influences in the characteristic environment of a port city inevitably gave rise to the area's own individual expressions of urban culture. Amongst these, the most notable is Fado, a musical form that was born in the popular quarters of Lisbon.

The links between Alfama and the port can be felt most acutely in the centre of the quarter, in the Square of Largo do Chafariz de Dentro. Its name derives from the fountain (*chafariz*) that can still be found there and once stood within (*dentro*) the old city walls, close to the Porta do Mar, the gate that opened onto the riverside district.

House of Fado and of the Portuguese Guitar, Lisbon.

In this square, in the building known as Recinto da Praia, the Casa do Fado e da Guitarra Portuguesa has been installed, a museological space of cultural entertainment devoted to Fado. Through a succession of atmospheres recreated by audio-visual means, visitors are invited to learn about the history of Fado, the places where music was played and how and where it was disseminated. A thorough investigation of Fado's cultural heritage is illustrated through musical revues, radio and recordings, as well as its later inclusion in the cinema and details about its great singers and instrumentalists. The route taken now through the narrow streets and arches of Alfama, from the castle perched on high to the Casa do Fado, is in fact the path followed by Lisbon's popular culture, deeply rooted in a centuries-old dialogue between races and cultures.

ITINERARY I   *Mudejar Art*
Sintra

I.2 SINTRA

Information Office: Praça da República, 23, tel: 21 923 11 57.

In countless descriptions provided by Arab geographers, Sintra is always mentioned as being dependent upon Lisbon. Apart from a number of other small settlements that took advantage of the fertile soil of the region's valleys, the main centres of population would have been the Moorish Castle and the area where the Vila Palace now stands. High up in the mountains, the long perimeter wall (heavily rebuilt as a result of Romanticism in the 19th century) defended a small set-

The Moorish Wall and Pena Palace, Sintra.

tlement and also served as a temporary refuge for those from outside. In view of its mild climate, leafy woods and abundant supplies of water, Sintra seems to have been favoured as a summer residence and leisure spot by the nobility of Lisbon, both before and after its inclusion in the kingdom of Portugal.

The Moorish community remained a very dense one throughout the region. At the end of the 15th century, there was still mention of a Moorish Cemetery in Colares, which D. Manuel I gave to a private individual.

At the height of the period of Romanticism that swept across Europe in the 19th century, Sintra joined in with the Revivalist movement. This resulted in the blending of many of the region's historical features with visions of an exotic East, which at that time was undergoing a process of conquest and assimilation by various colonial powers. The Pena Palace thus came into being as a work that reflected the wishes of a prince consort of German origin. Likewise, the Monserrate Pavilion would have made no sense without the Indian and Moorish delirium that inspired its creation and was so fashionable amongst British aristocratic circles at the time.

C. T.

I.2.a Vila Palace

Largo Rainha D. Amélia, tel: 21 910 68 40. Entrance fee. Open: 10.00-13.00 (last admissions at 12.30) and 14.00-17.00 (last admissions at 16.30); closed on Wednesdays and public holidays.

Surrounded by the houses of the present-day town of Sintra and occupying the whole of the top of a small hill overlooking one of the region's most luxuriant valleys, the palace stands out by virtue of the

ITINERARY I *Mudejar Art*
Sintra

Vila Palace, Sintra.

extraordinary interplay between its different volumes and shapes. In more remote times, this was a small, fortified settlement where the inhabitants of the surrounding region would seek refuge in the event of danger. In the Islamic period, although it continued to perform this same role for a brief period, this small fortification was almost certainly rebuilt at the end of the $5^{th}/11^{th}$ century to adapt the area between the walls for recreational purposes and to serve as a country residence. Although there is no actual archaeological evidence of this, such a conclusion is suggested by its systematic use by the queens of the first Portuguese Dynasty. Major rebuilding work was undertaken to transform the area into a palace in the 15th and 16th centuries, and Moorish taste is echoed in a whole series of additional volumes that have been interlaced and juxtaposed to achieve an architectural synthesis of rare harmony. Small courtyards with babbling water and the gentle polychrome effect created by the use of glazed tiles have given the palace's interior one of the most beautiful atmospheres in Mudejar art and in the whole of Portuguese architecture.

C. T.

Leave the town by the Estrada da Pena.

I.2.b **Pena Palace**

Estrada da Pena, 2 km. south of Sintra. There are minibuses from here to the Palace, tel: 21 910 53 40.
Entrance fee. Open: 10.00-17.00 (winter); 10.00-18.30 (summer: June-September); closed on Mondays and public holidays.

High up in the Sintra hills, where previously there stood the 16th-century Monastery of Nossa Senhora da Pena, D. Fernando II built his legendary palace. This has since become the symbol of the king's personality and the defining image of the spirit of Romanticism that was prevalent at that time.
After purchasing the convent in 1838, the king had simply intended to repair the original building, but he ended up build-

ITINERARY I *Mudejar Art*

Sintra

Pena Palace, Sintra.

ing a fortified palace that, in its first phase, had no overall guiding plan. However, roughly two years later, "His Majesty", decided, "that the Convent should be transformed into a fortified palace, following the mixed Arabian, or Manueline, style of its origins".

In 1842, after building strong outside walls crowned by an elegant arcade drawn straight from a neo-Moorish textbook, the king ordered the chapel yard to be enlarged. The area that is now referred to as the queen's terrace was made more extensive by constructing "elegant arcades" in the Arabian style in order to allow for the formation of loggias.

The entrance gate, which is immediately followed by a drawbridge, provides some information on the symbolism that underlines its function as an "antechamber".

This chamber was to prepare the visitor for an understanding of the dreamlike (or perhaps real) delirium of the portico, an allegory of the creation of the world, which is sited a little further up the hill in the noble façade of the "new palace".

The overall project was the work of the engineer Ludwige Eschwege, but the king significantly changed the decoration, giving the impression that the German's proposal had been cast aside.

The portico known as the "Triton Arch" or the "allegory of the creation of the world" displays heavy symbolism connected to life itself, whether this is understood in the physical or spiritual sense. This leads to the arcaded courtyard, displaying in its passageway, together with much exoticism, "an elegant ceiling of Arabian taste, imitating natural stalactites".

On part of the façade overlooking the courtyard is the famous window inspired by that found on the outer wall of the chapter house at the Convento de Cristo (Tomar). This window was certainly designed by D. Fernando and can now be considered as representing the very birth of the neo-Manueline style.

D. Fernando was not content simply to transpose this style to the Pena Palace, but instead produced an amalgam of Oriental, Moorish, Indian and maritime features, resulting in a compositional irregularity that is highly gratifying for those with a Romantic spirit.

The interior decoration of the palace seems to have been carried out without any specific programme. That said, the fact remains that, at that time, the prevailing fashion was for decorators to effect a contrast between the styles used in different compartments, and such eclecticism provided a vast range of options, even though it was always guided by a taste for comfort.

It was not by mere chance that D. Fernando's palace appeared in its present position crowning the rocks of Pena, and its emergence here has in fact to be understood in a much broader context.

M. R. A.

I.2.c **The Moorish Castle**

Estrada da Pena, Serra da Sintra, tel: 21 924 72 00.
Open: 9.30-17.00 (winter); 10.00-18.00 (summer); closed on 1st January and 25th December.

Pena Palace, Sintra.

The Moorish Castle, Sintra.

ITINERARY I   *Mudejar Art*

Sintra

Monserrate Palace, panoramic of the garden, Sintra.

Crowning the Sintra hills and covering an area of four hectares there can still be seen a long stretch of crenellated wall with rectangular turrets. Little now remains of this fortified settlement, which was still inhabited in the 5th/11th century and was certainly also used by shepherds and their flocks as a temporary shelter. The Prince Regent D. Fernando II, the same man who had rebuilt the nearby Pena Palace in the mid-19th century, was also the creator of the Romantic scenography that now surrounds these beautiful ruins. The battlements, steps and parapets were adapted to form a path that affords visitors the chance to enjoy extraordinarily beautiful views over the surrounding landscape.

C. T.

I.2.d Monserrate Palace and Gardens

Estrada de Monserrate, tel: 21 923 12 01.
It is only possible to visit the gardens, as the palace itself is closed.
Entrance fee. Open: 9.00-18.00 (from October to March closed at 17.00); closed on 1st January, Easter, 1st May and 25th December.

The small Gothic palace that once belonged to De Visme and Beckford gave rise, some years later, to the "barbarous orientalism now to be seen at Monserrate, built by Viscount Cook in a fit of Moorish delirium". When he set out to rebuild the old house, Francis Cook sought the collaboration of the London architect James T. Knowles Senior, who drew up the plans in 1858, leading to the appearance of a structure which was vaguely related to Moorish and Indian formulas.

The small oblong palace has a central cubical structure flanked by two round towers at either end, covered by elegant domes and reminiscent of stylised lotus flowers, a fact that affords them a strange exoticism. The openings in the white outside walls of Monserrate Palace contrast with these red domes and, above their lintels are ogival "fanlights", filled with filigreed stone arabesques.

The gallery that runs across the inside of the palace was once remarkably beautiful. Due to a system of natural lighting, that was quite sophisticated for the time, the arches follow on from one another and create areas of shadow and light that cause the rich stucco tracery to stand out in a quite surprising fashion.

When entering through the outside porch that looks out over the park in this capricious hallucination, and before reaching the octagonal lobby, visitors are obliged to pass through yet more fabulous stucco arches and thus to admire the finely decorated staircase leading to the upper floor. Immediately before the once truly breathtaking music room (to judge by the remains that can still be seen), there stood another dazzling room, previously lined with Venetian mirrors, with white marble fireplaces and fairy-tale chandeliers of Bohemian crystal.

In Monserrate, Sir Francis Cook did not merely limit himself to "erecting in an instant chimerical fantasies of architecture and sculpture" and "adorning the halls and galleries of that charming mansion with the most precious works of art", for he was also greatly concerned with the park and gardens. A scientific element was introduced into this latter area. Its mentors must have been William Colebrook Stockdale, the Romantic landscape artist who was a frequent visitor to Portugal, and Thomas Cargill, a Lisbon doctor and friend of the owner, who must in turn have been helped by William Nevril, a specialist in the field of botany. All of these men received the support of the English gardener Francis Burt, who died in Portugal in 1877.

The marvellous palatial residence of Monserrate achieves such perfect harmony with its extraordinary park that all those who have the privilege to see it find its charms difficult to resist.

M. R. A.

For Santarém, take the IC19 road back towards Lisbon and then follow the A1 motorway in the direction of Santarém / Porto.
For Alenquer, return to Lisbon and take the A1 motorway as far as Carregado, then follow the signs to Alenquer.
For Óbidos, follow the A9 / CREL motorway to Loures and then continue along the A8-IC1 road as far as Torres Vedras / Caldas da Rainha, coming off at Óbidos.

Natural Park of Sintra / Cascais
Only a stone's throw from Lisbon, the Natural Park of Sintra / Cascais is the first "cultural landscape" to have been classified as a World Heritage Site. Those who visit the area today find themselves going back in time to a period when human life was shaped by (or did itself shape) a diversified landscape full of unexpected charms.
The peculiar climate of the Serra de Sintra, the result of a curious volcanic eruption some 80 million years ago, keeps the mountains swathed in a permanent mist that has given rise to dense green vegetation, patiently worked by human hand. Sintra, which was known in classical times as "Mons Lunae" (The Mountain of the Moon), became the refuge of kings, poets, hermits and aristocrats, who built palaces, mansions, country houses, cottages, convents and chapels, surrounded by parks filled with plants brought from all four corners of the world.
To the north, human communities occupied the plains of important streams, building small groups of houses and dividing the landscape into vineyards, vegetable patches and orchards enclosed by dry-stone walls or hedges made from reeds and canes, later becoming known as the "saloio" region.
Along the coast, Cabo da Roca, the headland "where the land ends and the sea begins" is the westernmost point of continental Europe. Amongst the variety of botanical species that are to be found here, the Armeria, pseudarmeria *and* Silene cintrana *are exclusive to these rugged cliffs, over which fly sea birds and birds of prey, such as the crested cormorant and the peregrine falcon. It is still possible, on the coast, to find sandy beaches that have adapted to the*

ITINERARY I *Mudejar Art*
Alenquer

Castle, armory tower, Alenquer.

strong winds of the Guincho and Raso area and the fossil dunes of Magoito and Oitavos.
Sites not to be missed by any visitor to the Natural Park of Sintra / Cascais are the Convento dos Capuchos, Adega de Colares, Azenhas do Mar, and the road from Cabo da Roca to Praia da Adraga.

C. G. / P. N.

Tourist Information: Rua General Alves Roçadas, 10-2°, 2710 Sintra, tel: 21 923 51 16/66.

I.3 **ALENQUER** (option)

I.3.a Islamic Alenquer

Information: Tel: 263 73 09 00.
Museu Municipal Hipólito Cabaço, tel: 263 73 09 06.

In the Islamic period, the small town of Alenquer, built close to a navigable stretch of the River Tagus, was an integral part of the network of urban centres linked to Lisbon by an intense river traffic. With Arruda, Xira, Azambuja and Benavente, it shared the bread-producing region of Ballata, whose products were sold in the capital, benefiting and controlling all the trade routes from Coruche, Tomar or Santarém.

Because of a lack of archaeological information, it is not possible to infer that there was any structure here prior to the buildings evidently erected in the Low Middle Ages, particularly those dating from the period of the Renaissance, which left the region with a number of impressive monuments. On the walls of the *medina* – an enclosed and heavily populated area of roughly five hectares – a monumental for-

ITINERARY I *Mudejar Art*
Óbidos

tified tower can be seen, the base of which would almost certainly have been part of the Muslim defensive system.

Unlike the castle, whose foundations may perhaps be revealed only by future excavations, it is possible today for people to visit the city walls and the fortified tower associated with them. There is a small archaeological museum with a collection of ceramic artefacts, mainly from the 14th century, although there are also some from the Islamic period.

C. T.

For Óbidos, take the Estrada Nacional No. 9 to Torres Vedras, then join the A8-IC1 road to Óbidos, For Santarém, return to the A1 motorway and head north in the direction of Santarém / Porto.

I.4 ÓBIDOS (option)

I.4.a Historical town of Óbidos

Information: Rua Direita, tel: 262 95 92 31.

Before the widespread silting that was to transform the whole of Portugal's Atlantic coastline after the end of the Middle Ages, the lagoon known as Lagoa de Óbidos, which today is confined to the coastal area, would have reached almost to the foot of the hill. Here there was once a prosperous port flourishing beneath the shadow of the imposing castle and fortified town. In addition to a certain amount of archaeological evidence, the fact that the place-name of Óbidos derives directly from the

Castle and historical town of Óbidos.

ITINERARY I   *Mudejar Art*
Santarém

Castle and riverside, Santarém.

Latin term *opidum* suggests that there was once an earlier fortress on this site before the mediaeval structure seen today. Written documents refer to the town's conquest by the first king of Portugal some years before he took Lisbon, and it is clear that at that time the settlement was already enclosed by sturdy walls. Although there is no direct reference to the Islamic period – except possibly for a few stones at the base of the Torre do Facho – this town deserves a visit for its excellent quality whitewashed houses contained within its walls. All of this historical area, which has remained well preserved in terms of the original layout of its streets and architecture, has close connections with the Mediterranean tradition.

C. T.

Take the IP6 in the direction of Rio Maior and then continue along Estrada Nacional No. 114 to Santarém.

I.5 SANTARÉM

Information: Rua Capelo e Ivens, 63, tel: 243 30 44 37.

The city of Santarém (previously known as Scalabis, the capital of the Roman *conventus*) dominates the immense plains of the Ribatejo, the former territory of Ballata, which had been referred to and praised by both Roman and Arab chroniclers. The river continuously flooded the land here and the farming techniques used

ITINERARY I   *Mudejar Art*
Santarém

were compared by the chronicler al-Himyari to those used on the mud flats of the River Nile.
Apparently, Santarém was organised into three quite distinct nuclei. The citadel was certainly protected by a wall and had three gates, continuing as far as the area of São João de Alporão. Close to the River Tagus and around the church dedicated to Saint Irene, the city's patron saint, there spread the suburb of Alfange and in particular the suburb of Ribeira, which formed the most important nucleus of the Islamic city.
Due to the continuation of this important Christian cult, as proved by the very name of the city (Xantarin), a sizeable Mozarab population was to remain, particularly in the riverside areas.

C. T.

I.5.a **Santarém Municipal Museum - São João de Alporão**

Largo Zeferino Sarmento, tel: 243 30 44 40. Entrance fee. Open: 9.30-12.30 and 14.00-17.30; closed on Mondays and public holidays.

In São João de Alporão, there are three remarkable architectural capitals, which have been carefully documented since the end of the 19th century. Two of them can be attributed to the period of the *caliphs* and the other to the Almoravid period. The older ones are finely carved pieces,

Capital of White Marble, 6th/12th century, Santarém Municipal Museum, São João de Alporão.

where it is possible to note a progression in the use of geometric patterns, based upon classical references such as Corinthian volutes and acanthus leaves. The abacus, however, begins to reveal the use of a complex and progressively more abstract tracery. This decorative system makes it possible to suggest that these pieces be from a period after the rule of the *caliphs*, so that they are probably from the 6th/12th century. In view of the cartouches and their religious inscriptions, these capitals must once have belonged to a mosque, of which they now remain as the only testimony.

C. T.

ITINERARY II

Between Moors and Mozarabs

Cláudio Torres, Maria Adelaide Miranda, Mário Pereira, Santiago Macias

II.1 COIMBRA
        II.1.a National Museum of Machado de Castro
        II.1.b Almedina Gate
        II.1.c Islamic Walls and City

II.2 LORVÃO
        II.2.a Monastery

        The Lorvão Apocalypse

II.3 LOUROSA
        II.3.a Parish Church of Lourosa

II.4 AVÔ (option)
        II.4.a Castle

II.5 PIÓDÃO (option)
        II.5.a Village

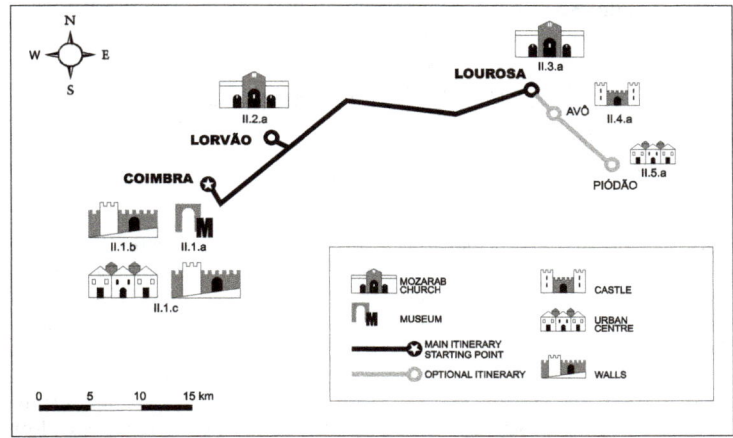

Parish Church of San Pedro, Lourosa.

ITINERARY II   Between Moors and Mozarabs

Coimbra

National Museum of Machado de Castro, Mozarabe's door, Coimbra.

The Mondego river, an old inlet from the sea, and the fertile marshes around the city of Coimbra that extend as far as the fortress of Montemor, form a perfectly coherent territory, a kind of Mediterranean island amidst the undulating mountains functioning as a buttress against the central Iberian system. The fields of the Mondego Valley were crossed in a north-south direction by the road that connected the cities of Porto and Braga to the Tagus valley and were always sufficient to feed a highly sedentary population, little given to accepting hurried changes imposed by their conquerors. This explains why, during the periods of Muslim influence, the people of this region remained stubbornly *Mozarab*. It also helps us to understand their strong attachment to Mediterranean traditions when subjected to military occupation by the feudal lords from the rugged northern mountains. The people of Coimbra seem to have been successful in negotiating and maintaining their autonomy at a time of the military campaigns waged by Islamic armies. Later on, at the beginning of the 12th century, when the region was already subject to the Christian domination imposed by the papal hierarchy, the local population engaged in violent urban rebellions in an attempt to impose their traditions of *Mozarab* worship. On the fertile plains of the Mondego and along the sheltered hillsides and valleys of its tributaries, the population retained their strong Mediterranean and Islamic traditions, reflected both in the place names and eating habits, as well as in the weaving and building techniques.

It was in this city and its surrounding region that a synthesis of two civilisations from north and south was achieved. It was here to a certain extent that the fleeting spirit of tolerance was created that presided over the formation of the Kingdom of Portugal.

C. T.

II.1 COIMBRA

Information: Largo da Portagem, tel: 239 85 59 30.

This was how the Arab chronicler al-Razi described the city of the Mondego Valley in the $4^{th}/10^{th}$ century: "The city of Coimbra is very strong: it is a most excellent castle. It is situated upon the Mondego, which has its source in the mountains of Serra da Estrela and passes at the foot of various castles that depend on

ITINERARY II Between Moors and Mozarabs
Coimbra

Coimbra. This river rushes into the sea 24 miles from Coimbra; it abounds in fish of many species. The city of Coimbra is beautiful and endowed with different riches; on the banks of the river it has a plain that is very good for crops, even without irrigation. When the river comes out of its bed, the plain is entirely covered. Later, when the river retreats, so well is the grain sown that the inhabitants harvest wheat enough for the whole year and for the following year, although the plain is no more than 15 miles long and 4 miles wide. The city of Coimbra has many orchards with good yields and numerous olive-groves that provide very good oil. Coimbra is a very ancient land." Coimbra may be considered as the northernmost city with Mediterranean characteristics in the west of the Iberian Peninsula and, in Islamic times, it covered a walled area of roughly 10 hectares inhabited by some three to four thousand people. Built on a hill overlooking the plains of the Mondego Valley, its territory stretched as far as the sea, close to which there stood the imposing fortress of Montemor-o-Velho.

A monumental citadel, with an adjoining residential quarter, that dominated the top of the hill, where the old university and its campus of modern faculties now stands. Close to the river, along the top of the road that led to the north, there developed a heavily populated quarter of fishermen, traders and artisans, to which access was gained through the Porta de Almedina.

C. T.

II.1.a **National Museum of Machado de Castro**

Largo Dr. José Rodrigues, tel: 239 82 37 27. Entrance fee. Open: 9.00-12.30 (last admissions at 12.00) and 14.00-17.30 (last admissions at 17.00); closed on Mondays and public holidays.

This important national museum housed in the former Episcopal Palace stands on an artificial platform created by a monumental Roman forum. Beside being one of the most significant collections of Christian art in Portugal, the museum exhibits a well-preserved capital, with

Coimbra.

ITINERARY II   *Between Moors and Mozarabs*
Coimbra

National Museum of Machado de Castro, Mozarabe's door, Coimbra.

finely sculpted tracery that is unmistakably from the period of the *Caliph*s (4th/10th-5th/11th centuries). At the same place, and also originating from the castle at Montemor-o-Velho, are two fragments of a plaster-of-Paris and lime decoration, with motifs similar to those found at the Aljaferia in Zaragoza and dating from the 5th/11th century. Another capital with Corinthian volutes, also from the period of the *Caliph*s and originating from the same fortified settlement, is now exhibited at Évora Museum, where it was taken at the end of the 19th century.

C. T.

The *Mozarab* Gate

After the city had been conquered in 456/1064 and integrated into the Condado Portucalense (the County of Portugal), there nonetheless remained a strong *Mudejar* community in the area whose power was only definitively brought under control at the end of 5th -b. 6th/b. 12th century. The capacity and prestige of this group certainly had a decisive influence upon local taste. The supposed double gate of the old Episcopal Palace – which would have performed similar functions in an earlier defensive wall built around the Islamic city – was certainly remodelled after the Christian Reconquest. With its clearly defined horseshoe arches contained within an *alfiz*, the gate displays the architectural aesthetics typically found in the Maghreb empires of the time.

C. T.

Walk along Rua Borges Carneiro, pass through Largo da Sé Velha and continue the descent along Rua do Quebra-Costas until you reach the Arco de Almedina.

II.1.b Almedina Gate

Rua do Quebra-Costas.

The main gate leading to the *medina* opened directly onto the river, whose navigable channel stretched at the time as far as the present-day Rua Ferreira Borges. In the area known as Portagem, an old Roman bridge (now buried by sand) carried the road that crossed the river and linked Lisbon to the north. On the side walls of this gate, which still affords access to the inner city even today, it is possible to see, close to the 17th-century vaulting, the springers of two imposing horseshoe arches that framed the original double gateway into the Muslim city. The passage of time, the desire to erase the marks left by the defeated population and the need for new building work have meant that the imposts that jutted out from the arches have been removed, giving them their present-day semicircular appearance.

C. T.

II.1.c **Islamic Walls and City**

The growth of Coimbra, immediately after the Low Middle Ages, together with the massive destruction caused in the 20th century by the construction of university buildings at the top of the city, have made it difficult to read the topography of the Islamic city.
The walls that surrounded Coimbra in the Islamic period stretched along Couraça de Lisboa, passing close to Rua Ferreira Borges (next to which is the Almedina Gate) and then climbed upwards to the area around the present-day Museu Nacional de Machado de Castro. Further up the hill, the area now occupied by Largo de D. Dinis would have been the site of the citadel.
The Islamic cemetery was perhaps located to the north of the walls, on the site where the Sé Nova (New Cathedral) was later built.

S. M.

The Inscription in the Old Cathedral

Largo da Sé Velha, tel: 239 82 52 73.
Entrance fee to cloister. Closed on Fridays.

In the north wall of the Sé Velha (Old Cathedral), it is still possible to see an inscription in Arabic, which is clearly contemporary with the cathedral's actual construction and dates from the 6th/12th century. "I wrote this as a permanent record of my suffering. My hand will perish one day, but the grandeur will remain", this was the lament of an unknown stonemason obliged to perform such a painful task, but who, nonetheless, betrayed his admiration for the splendour of the work and was certainly already motivated to accept an inevitable religious assimilation. Many other Moorish stonemasons and craftsmen remained in the city to contribute to the growth of the new capital of the nascent Kingdom of Portugal.

C. T.

Almedina Gate, Coimbra.

ITINERARY II *Between Moors and Mozarabs*
Lorvão

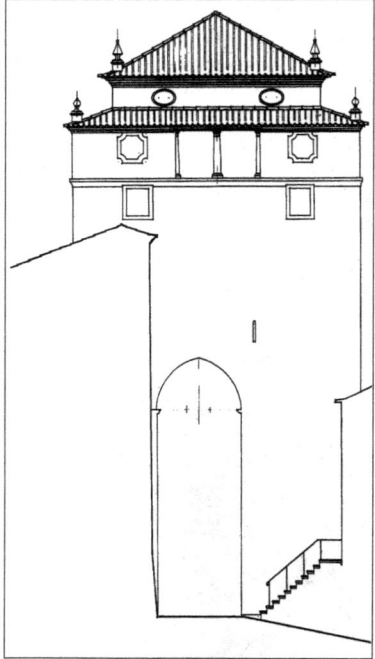

Almedina Gate, northern façade, according to the DGEMN's drawing, Coimbra.

Take the IP3 towards Viseu, turn left to Penacova and continue on to Lorvão.

II.2 **LORVÃO**

II.2.a **Monastery**

Open: 9.00-12.30 and 14.00-17.30 (winter); 9.00-12.30 and 14.00-18.30 (summer; June-September); closed on Mondays and Tuesdays.

Lorvão Monastery, dedicated to São Pelágio and São Mamede, is one of the monasteries that still contains documentary evidence and artistic remains of its Mozarab past. The date of its foundation is uncertain. The *Crónica de Cister* points to the 6th century as the most probable date, a hypothesis that has recently been strengthened by the discovery of a stone attributed to the Visigothic period on the site of the monastery. However, the dating suggested by Bernardo de Brito was called into question by means of a rigorous criticism made of the documentary sources by Rui de Azevedo, who has himself set the approximate date for the founding of the monastery at 878.

There is data available about life at the monastery since the 10th century, after the capture of Coimbra by Alfonso III of León. The oldest known fact relates to the donation of the area of Vila Cova by Ordonho II in 911. These donations continued and, during this same century, the monastery expanded and became one of those that were protected by the Counts of Coimbra. Its importance was also justified by the prestige afforded to the cult of São Mamede and the political crisis of the Leonese monarchy, which gave the monastery greater autonomy. During the Islamic period, the importance of Coimbra grew with the river trade that brought greater vitality to the whole area, with Lorvão being situated on one of the major trade routes for the transport of coal, firewood and timber. In 966, an important event occurred in the history of the monastery when the abbot, Abade Primo, called in Zacarias, the master builder of bridges and roads, from Córdoba. Together with the abbot, the latter was responsible for many important building works at the monastery.

In the 11th century, the monastery lost some of its prestige due to the popularity of the shrine of São Vicente da Vacariça, although from 1086 onwards it was to recover most of its property and assets. Like most monasteries in the North East of the Iberian Peninsula, it was probably

ITINERARY II *Between Moors and Mozarabs*
Lorvão

Monastery of Lorvão.

influenced by the Fructuosian Rule, being somewhat late in adopting the Rule of St. Benedict and, with the support of D. Afonso Henriques and his daughter D. Teresa, joining the Order of Cistercian nuns in 1200.

It was at this monastery that one of the most fundamental manuscripts for the study of illuminated works in Portugal was produced, the now famous *Apocalipse do Lorvão* (Lorvão Apocalypse).

M. A. M.

Return to the IP3, heading towards Viseu, and then take the IC7 in the direction of Arganil / Oliveira do Hospital. Continue along Estrada Nacional No. 17 to Venda da Esperança and then turn right to Lourosa (about 50 km.).

THE LORVÃO APOCALYPSE

Maria Adelaide Miranda

The Lorvão Apocalipse, lighting, 12th century, National Archives of Torre do Tombo.

This commentary on the Apocalypse was produced at Lorvão Monastery and can now be found at the National Archives of Torre do Tombo. It was copied by Egeias in 1189, has 219 folios and is written in two columns, measuring 345 x 245 mm. on a parchment support. It is a late work, belonging to the so-called *Beatus,* a series of commentaries on the Apocalypse that originated in an 8th-century copy, written and illuminated by Beatus, a monk from Liebana. This series of roughly 25 manuscripts contains iconography that displays the concerns and anxieties experienced just before the end of the Millennium. The *Apocalipse do Lorvão* consists of 70 stories accompanied by their respective illustrations. The illuminator produced his compositions in a particularly original manner. The characters float in a virtual space, which is abstract because it is holy, in strips with geometrical backgrounds that are always laden with great symbolism. The manuscript presents features that are extremely important for establishing points of contact with Mozarab illumination. As is shown by the iconography which is similar, the copy was made on top of an older manuscript which is attributed to Beatus of Liebana himself (fragment of Silos) and belonged to the I family, to which the Beatus of Osma also belonged. The Mozarab period is equally visible in the architecture of the surmounted arch used by the artist.

It is the only Portuguese manuscript from that period, in which the predominant feature is its symbolic narrative aspect and where the representation of the human figure occupies a great deal of space.

II.3 LOUROSA

II.3.a Parish Church of Lourosa

The church can only be visited in the company of Maria Patrocínio Nunes, who can be contacted locally or by telephone at 232 81 66 21.

There is no doubt about the date of the foundation of this austere rural church (299/ 912), which not only serves as a chronological reference for all the transitional architecture of the central region, but also represents the most significant Mozarab monument in Portugal. Despite a number of Asturian references in the church's rustic engravings, the influences of the architectural models favoured by the Andalusian emirs are clearly visible in the modulation of the masonry and mainly in the decorative elements of the cornices and the design of the arches. The parish church of São Pedro de Lourosa is a building of the basilican type, in which a small transept separates the chancel from the main body of the building, where a row of three surmounted arches supported on columns separates the central nave from the side aisles.
During the restoration work carried out in the mid-20th century, when the entire building was restored to its original design, various architectural features were found that would have belonged to another earlier Visigothic church.
A cemetery was discovered in the churchyard with tombs that had been carved out of the rock, a sacrificial altar and other indications of the continued occupation of the site.

C. T.

Parish Church of San Pedro, exterior, Lourosa.

Parish Church of San Pedro, interior, Lourosa.

Avô

Return to Estrada Nacional No. 17 and head back to Venda de Galizes, turning right towards Avô along Estrada Nacional No. 230.

II.4 AVÔ (option)

II.4.a Castle

On the banks of the River Alva, the town of Avô occupies a strategic position overlooking the fertile valley and enjoying excellent natural conditions for its defence and domination.

The castle played an important role at the time, with a constantly shifting frontier between the Christian North and the Islamic South. The pointed arch and some sections of wall define what was once a walled area that naturally earned the attention of the first kings of Portugal as a means of settling the population in one place and consolidating the frontier.

Count D. Henrique gave Avô to the Bishop of Coimbra, who thereafter became the *alcaide* and lord of the castle.

There are some reports suggesting that this castle was the scene of some important battles during the struggle between D. Sancho II and Alfonso III.

It is curious to note that there is also a space here which bears the name of Couraça. Just as in Coimbra (Couraça de Lisboa) or Estremoz (Torre das Couraças), it indicates a protected access to water, vital for the continued resistance of the residents and their neighbours, who sought refuge inside the castle walls.

In the town, which received its first charter from D. Sancho I in 1178, later renewed in 1514 by D. Manuel I, there is still an invocation to be found of São Miguel (in the chapel next to the walls). Just like the Moura river this provides yet one more example of how local place names endure, to some extent, to preserve the legacy of an Islamic presence. The old town hall and Manueline pillory are other remains that testify to the importance of this town in earlier times.

M. R.

Returning to Estrada Nacional No. 230, head for Vide, where, immediately after crossing the bridge, turn right and head towards Piódão (roughly 16 km.).

II.5 PIÓDÃO (option)

Information: Avenida das Forças Armadas, Arganil, tel: 235 20 48 23.

II.5.a Village

Nightfall in Piódão is an unforgettable experience for those who have had the chance to see it. Here the presence of nature is felt in a uniquely intense manner, against a stark backdrop of mountains, water and schist.

Castle, Avô.

ITINERARY II   Between Moors and Mozarabs
Piódão

Urban residential area, Piódão.

The mountains have determined the layout of the town. Small, narrow streets wind their way up the hillside and form a mass of houses that have been built specifically to look out over the valley. Schist is used to pave the streets in different ways and this allows the torrents of water to run off them when it rains, making it possible for people to circulate with greater comfort. The compositions of these pavements are marked by a great sensuality in their shapes. Schist is an ever-present feature of the village. We find it on the roads and pavements, in the dividing walls between properties, the walls and roofs of houses, the roofs of the mills and other farm buildings.

Even today, the village still displays a remarkable unity in its layout, appearing as a group of houses built on terraces but blending together to form one of the best examples of the harmonious dialogue between man and nature.

It is an excellent example of the Portuguese rural heritage – clearly displaying how the wisdom of local experience has been put to use to find the most efficient solutions for taking advantage of everything that nature has to offer.

M. P.

Alcántara (Spain)
On the other side of the frontier, in Spanish Estremadura, it is well worth taking the time to travel to the beautiful town of Trujillo, which is still dominated today by one of the most important and monumental fortresses from the period of the caliphs. When passing through Cáceres, it is also recommended that visitors spend some time at the regional museum housed in the Casa de las Veletas built on top of an Islamic cistern. On returning to the Portuguese border at Segura, you will cross the River Tagus by the famous Roman Bridge, at Alcántara.

C. T.

ITINERARY III

Idanha: Border Country

Cláudio Torres, Mário Pereira, Cristina Garcia, Paula Noronha

III.1 IDANHA-A-VELHA
   III.1.a Castle and Village
   III.1.b Cathedral
      (a former mosque)

III.2 MONSANTO
   III.2.a Castle

III.3 SABUGAL (option)
   III.3.a Castle

III.4 SORTELHA (option)
   III.4.a Castle

III.5 ALFAIATES (option)
   III.5.a Castle

III.6 CASTELO DE VIDE
   III.6.a Islamic Castelo de Vide

III.7 MARVÃO
   III.7.a Castle and Town

III.8 CRATO (option)
   III.8.a Town

III.9 ALTER DO CHÃO (option)
   III.9.a Castle

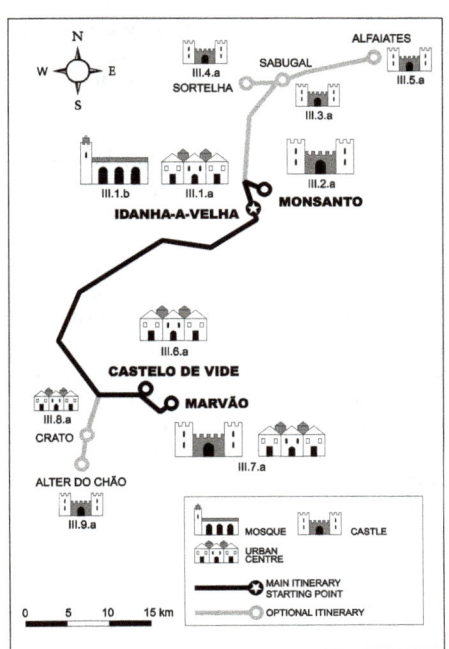

Castelo of Vide, detail, 16th-century drawing, in Duarte d'Armas, "Livro das Fortalezas".

Idanha: Border Country

Castle, Sortelha.

In the early days of Islamicisation, the great cities and fertile plains of the coastal region and the Alentejo rapidly adapted to the new social and religious order. In the valleys and hilly outcrops to the north of the river Tagus, other problems were faced. These problems did not spring particularly from the constant waves of military conquests and reconquests, as one might imagine. They can be attributed more to the natural restraint and mistrust of the shepherd folk in the area, for whom the assimilation of new ideas from the south was not only a slow, laborious process, but also one that lacked any real rigour in technical and liturgical terms. This phenomenon sometimes allowed for sudden outbursts of innovation, which has always been the hallmark of the border areas, where controls are frequently stricter and interchanges therefore more imaginative.

In these inland mountain regions, where the roads were always rough and dangerous, the only major connection between the Asturias and the Mediterranean ports continued to be the Via da Prata (the Silver Way), which, in Roman times, linked Astorga and León to the cities of Mérida and Seville. This was the road onto which there converged the various routes of access to the castles and fortified villages that, in the immediate vicinity of the present-day Portuguese border, served as a refuge for the native peasants and shepherds. Although there is no conclusive archaeological evidence, there are, however, some local indications that suggest that there was a certain ancient dependence of this region, which was subject to the payment of tributes to the Islamic world of the south. This is the case with the Castle of Alfaiates, the origin of whose name has nothing to do with the prosaic activity of cutting and sewing (in Portuguese, *alfaiate* means tailor). In fact, the place name *al-hajar* was commonly used for fortifications built in the Islamic period, as in Arabic it means "stones" or "crags". This region along the north-south frontier proved to be a major battleground for skirmishes between Moors and Christians until the $6^{th}/12^{th}$ century. Other military tensions were reconfirmed later during the 14th century, this time running along another border between east and west, when the period of systematic confrontation began between the kingdoms of Portugal and Castile, who fought for possession of the castles of the Ribacôa region.

C. T.

ITINERARY III   *Idanha: Border Country*
Idanha-a-Velha

Walls, Idanha-a-Velha.

III.1 IDANHA-A-VELHA

III.1.a Castle and Village

Information: Rua da Senhora do Almortão, Idanha-a-Nova, tel: 277 20 29 00.

Today, Idanha-a-Velha is a small village with only a few dozen inhabitants. And yet, the small country houses have either been superimposed onto the remains of ancient monuments or else they exhibit re-used building materials. This once important Roman City, known at that time as Egitania, was the See of a diocese throughout the period of Visigothic rule from Toledo. According to Ibn Hajjan, the Cordoban chronicler, during the first years of the Islamicisation process the old city was known as N.yani. He relates that it was the refuge for the locally born rebel Ibn Marwan and his clan, who had, for several decades, opposed the centralisation of power in the hands of the *Caliph*s of Cordoba.

The solid granite masonry walls that still encircle Idanha even today are of the same type as those found at the Conventual in Mérida (built in 219/835). Chronologically, these walls were either slightly earlier than, or even perhaps contemporary with, the defences of Talavera de la Reina, built at the orders of Abd al-Rahman III at the end of 3rd-b. 4th/b. 10th century. As in the case of the latter, the semi-cylindrical turrets found in Idanha are part of a Roman and Byzantine tradition. The city's northern gate, with its double entrance flanked by two semi-cylindrical towers, also points to a similar chronology.

C. T.

III.1.b Cathedral (a former mosque)

Considered for many years as a Visigothic Cathedral, this church can today be classified as a mosque, or at least as a building with syncretic characteristics. The vaulted chapel exhibits the customary concern with ensuring that the mosque pointed towards Mecca, although, because of its size, it has little to do with the traditional *mihrab*. A

General view, Idanha-a-Velha.

ITINERARY III   Idanha: Border Country
Monsanto

Cathedral (former mosque), outside, Idanha-a-Velha.

Cathedral (former mosque), inside, Idanha-a-Velha.

row of slightly surmounted arches, forming a transverse nave, clearly causes this chapel to stand out from the rest of the architecture. Allowing for the fact that the south-eastern wall is the *qibla* of a mosque, the abnormal and disoriented arrangement of the building's dimensions becomes less enigmatic. The building of this strange mosque can only be attributed to a period of great disturbance when power was in the hands of the *muladi* rebel Ibn Marwan (towards the end of the $3^{rd}/9^{th}$ century). In order to establish such a chronological assertion, a number of features that seem significant should be considered. The most evident of all these parallels is that between the building techniques used at the Mosque in Idanha and those found at Lourosa Parish Church, little more than 70 km. away, which has an inscription with the date of 299/912.

C. T.

For Monsanto, follow Estrada Nacional No. 332 in the direction of Medelim / Penamacor and turn right before Medelim, following Estrada Nacional No. 239 to the crossroads for Monsanto.

III.2 **MONSANTO**

III.2.a Castle

Information: Rua Marquês da Graciosa, tel: 277 31 46 42.

From whichever direction one approaches Monsanto, it is easy to understand how the hill gained its name (Monte Santo - Sacred Hill).
This is a hill that stands out from the rest, a hill that draws people to it, a hill that deserves to be made sacred!
The excellence of this particular site first began to attract settlers a long time ago. These early inhabitants ended up fortifying the hilltop, probably in pre-Roman times, and the dominion of this site was thereafter much coveted by Romans, Goths, Arabs and the Knights Templar. Names such as those of the Roman praetor Lucius Emilius Paulus, Gualdim Pais and the Count of Lippe, are linked to this castle, which continued to maintain its

ITINERARY III   *Idanha: Border Country*
Monsanto

strategic importance from ancient times to the period of the Peninsular Wars in the 19th century. This is borne out by the description and survey carried out by Eusébio Furtado, a Major of the Royal Engineering Corps (1813), which shows us a military fortress that was still perfectly operational at the time.

The site remained important during different historical periods and the castle clearly shows this evolution in the successive transformations that it has undergone. The mediaeval settlement spread around the citadel, which in this particular case had been given the name of Alvacara, and this area too was later encircled by walls. In the 16th century, Duarte D'Armas – author of a remarkable book that illustrates a few cities and fortified castles in Portugal – presented a settlement that was moving progressively closer to the cultivated fields at the foot of the hill. A mediaeval fortification that underwent several adaptations in its transitional phase and was later strengthened with bulwarks, the castle remains as a testimony to all its many transformations. Towers, mediaeval walls and battlements from the transitional phase coexist with the earthworks, gunpowder store and embrasures of the modern fortifications. The Pião watchtower and the Chapels of São-Pedro de Vir-a-Corça and São Miguel are the finest mediaeval testimonies to survive the explosion that destroyed the gunpowder store in 1815, along with a significant part of the structures that existed between the walls. In common with most citadels, the Church of Santa Maria do Castelo marks the passage from one form of worship to another, underlining the perpetuation of the site's sacredness and remaining as the symbol of the military victory of Christianity.

M. P.

Castle, Monsanto.

For Castelo de Vide, take Estrada Nacional No. 239 towards Proença-a-Velha and then continue along Estrada Nacional No. 233 to Escalos de Cima. Turn right towards Alcains and then take the IP2 towards Castelo Branco / Portalegre. Come off the IP2 at Alpalhão and follow Estrada Nacional No. 246 to Castelo de Vide.

Village, Monsanto.

ITINERARY III   *Idanha: Border Country*
Sabugal

Castle, Sabugal.

For Sabugal, take Estrada Nacional No. 239, turn left, pass through Medelim and then follow Estrada Nacional No. 332 towards Penamacor. From here continue along Estrada Nacional No. 233 to Sabugal.

III.3 SABUGAL

III.3.a Castle

Information: City Hall, Praça da República, tel: 271 75 10 40.
Open: 9.00-12.30 and 14.00-18.00 (in the summer the castle closes at 19.00).

In mediaeval terms, Sabugal Castle can be considered a fort.
With an irregular quadrangular shape, surrounded by a solid-looking pentagonal barbican and protected by dozens of embrasures (which, in the 16th century, allowed for the use of firearms), this castle is made even more imposing by the thickness and height of its perimeter walls. It also has an imposing defensive capacity afforded by its four sturdy square towers, two round turrets and impressive pentagonal keep. The keep is 28 m. high, with machicolation galleries on every side, various types of loopholes, different vaulted levels (with intersecting pointed arches), crowned with pyramid-shaped merlons. It is popularly known as the Torre das Cinco Quinas (the Five-Cornered Tower) due to its pentagonal base.
All in all it is a very imposing castle. It is also one of the castles of the Ribacôa region which came under the rule of the Portuguese crown with the signing of the Treaty of Alcanices in 1297, so that it is not therefore surprising that its construction date is attributed to the reign of D. Dinis. The picture drawn by Duarte D'Armas in the 16th century shows us a castle that is quite similar to the one that is still to be seen today and highlights its longstanding strategic importance – the control of a major crossing point on the River Côa. Its proximity to

ITINERARY III   Idanha: Border Country
Sortelha

the frontier meant that during the War of Independence in the 16th and 17th centuries, attempts were made to keep it operational. However, new defensive strategies relegated it to a secondary position, largely because of its geographical proximity to another great fortification that had meanwhile begun to take shape in Almeida.

It is quite easy to identify the wall that came out from and then returned to the citadel, leaving the pillory outside the Porta da Vila, just as it was represented by D'Armas in the 16th century.

M. P.

For Castelo de Vide, take Estrada Nacional No. 233 to Castelo Branco. Then follow the IP2 towards Portalegre, as far as Alpalhão. From here, follow Estrada Nacional No. 246 to Castelo de Vide.

Heading south from Sabugal, turn right towards Sortelha, roughly 12 km. away.

III.4 SORTELHA

III.4.a **Castle**

Information: City Hall of Sabugal, Praça da República, tel: 271 75 10 40.

Whenever a Portuguese example of a fortified mediaeval town is sort, Sortelha immediately springs to mind as one of the most typical instances of how such a space would be occupied, how its defensive structure would be built and how it would then spread outwards beyond the castle walls. Also typical is the location of the citadel, around which the settlement grew, protecting itself further with the building of an outer wall and towers that, in some cases, flanked and protected the entrances to the town.

It is interesting to note how everything here developed in accordance with the strict canons of mediaeval fortification.

Castle, Sortelha.

85

ITINERARY III   Idanha: Border Country

Alfaiates

Castle, Alfaiates.

The entrance to the citadel is through a gateway that is heavily protected by a machicolation gallery. Inside the walls, the cistern, the inaccessible keep with its raised entrance, and a false gate (leading to the valley on the opposite side from the village) all form part of a precinct where the marks of the wooden floors are still visible. The measurements that were used between the walls are engraved in the town walls, at the Porta Nova (New Gate), which faces towards the Serra da Estrela and through which there passes a well preserved mediaeval cobbled street. The Manueline pillory with its armillary sphere, the town hall and parish church (with its Mudejar roof) form the structural backbone of a settlement consisting of a number of small squares along a central street linking the two main gates.
The town and castle were built over several reigns, with evidence of construction work from the time of D. Sancho I, 1181, D. Sancho II, 1228, and, of course, D. Dinis, to the reign of D. Manuel I, in the 16th century. The embrasures, already designed for the use of firearms, date from this last period. Both the chapels of Santiago and São Genásio, the leper (indicating an ancient leper hospital) and the Quinta da Corredoura (where cattle passed through on their journey of transhumance) are clear reminders of the past history of this border settlement. An important watchtower in the hermitage of São Cornélio, overlooked the town.
One should also note the survival of the Capeia Raiana, representing a singular way of dealing with the bulls that are brought to the village in the summer for the traditional festivities in the Largo do Corro, next to the Porta da Vila.

M. T.

For Alfaiates, return on the same road to Sabugal and then follow Estrada Nacional No. 233-3 to Alfaiates.

For Castelo de Vide, follow Estrada Nacional No. 18-3 in the direction of Caria / Covilhã to the crossroads with the IP2 and then head along this road in the direction of Portalegre, coming off at Alpalhão. From here, take Estrada Nacional No. 246 to Castelo de Vide.

III.5 **ALFAIATES** (option)

III.5.a **Castle**

Information: City Hall of Sabugal, Praça da República, tel: 271 75 10 40.

For most of us, any mention of the Castle of Alfaiates is largely a reference to what is still visible and dates back to the period of Manueline rebuilding work, as shown by the heraldic device above the entrance to the fortified area. Little now remains of the original construction from the time of D. Dinis.

Existing documentation identifies the present-day Castle of Alfaiates with the changes introduced to the building by D. Manuel I, who ordered the town to be fortified in 1510.

Alfaiates provides a typical example of the transition from a mediaeval castle to a modern fortification, as is also true at Évoramonte or the Torre de Belém in Lisbon. Diogo de Arruda (1525) also built a defensive structure here, based primarily on the use of firearms. He is responsible for the quadrangular shape of this construction, with three circular corner towers and embrasures protecting the whole of the fortified area.

The original town of Alfaiates still has an interesting series of monuments: besides the castle, there are also the pillory and the Igreja da Misericórdia with its portals, corbelling and interesting Romanesque rose-window, as well as the Convento de Sacaparte, a most intriguing space that is full of legends.

M. P.

For Castelo de Vide, return to Sabugal and take Estrada Nacional No. 233 to Castelo Branco. After this, take the IP2 in the direction of Portalegre, coming off at Alpalhão. From here, take Estrada Nacional No. 246 to Castelo de Vide.

III.6 CASTELO DE VIDE

III.6.a **Islamic Castelo de Vide**

Information: tel: 245 90 13 61.

Castelo de Vide.

ITINERARY III   *Idanha: Border Country*
Marvão

Castelo de Vide.   *Urban residential area, Marvão.*

In the Islamic period, Castelo de Vide was a small hilltop settlement whose inhabitants would have been mainly shepherds. Today, it is a prosperous town, surrounded by verdant woodland and good farming land, with its modern development being largely the result of cross-border trade. The castle walls were certainly built or repaired at the end of the 14th century, mainly due to the insecurity of the border region, but also with the aim of protecting the prosperous Jewish community that had settled in the town. The most important feature of this beautiful Alentejo town is its urban layout and the exceptional series of stone door posts and lintels and Gothic arches, which make it the most interesting and best preserved mediaeval town in this region.

C. T.

Leave Castelo de Vide by Estrada Nacional No. 246-1, heading towards Marvão, roughly 13 km. away.

III.7 **MARVÃO**

III.7.a **Castle and Town**

Information: tel: 245 99 38 86.

Marvão is a fortified mediaeval town perched on top of a formidable rocky crag almost 1000 m. high. It is certainly one of the oldest settlements in the region. Legend attributes its foundation to the Muslim Lord of Coimbra, by the name of Marwan. In fact, this character is a well-known figure in the history of al-Andalus. The *muladi* Ibn Marwan al-Jilliqui (Marwan the Galician) was the leader of the local resis-

ITINERARY III   *Idanha: Border Country*
Crato

tance to the centralisation of power that had been initiated by the *Caliph*s of Cordoba in the second half of the 3rd/11th century. For almost a century, his clan led various rebellions of Gharb al-Andalus against the power of the *caliph*s, building themselves strong fortifications alternately at Badajoz, Idanha or Marvão. Given the strategic quality of this fortress, and therefore its longstanding and systematic settlement, the name of Marvão is probably not an ingenuous anthroponym. Instead it is probably this same family, who originated from and ruled over these lands, that adopted it as their surname and thus as a symbol of their regional power.

The landscape seen from the castle walls is quite breathtaking and, as its inhabitants frequently say, it is the only place where a birdseye view of flying kites can be enjoyed.

C. T.

Castle, Marvão.

Leave Marvão by Estrada Nacional No. 359 in the direction of Portalegre and then take Estrada Nacional No. 119 to Crato.

III.8 **CRATO** (option)

III.8.a **Town**

Information: Rua 5 de Outubro, tel: 245 99 71 61. Flor da Rosa, tel: 245 99 73 41.

After the Christian "Reconquest" at the end of 6th-b. 7th/b. 13th century, the Hospitallers were entrusted by the Portuguese king with the task of building the headquarters of their Order in this region. In Crato, they replaced what was possibly a citadel by building a fortified palace, of which little now remains, after the battles fought during the war of Restoration in the mid-17th century. Close by, there stands a restored building belonging to that same Order, the monumental Flor da Rosa Monastery.

Urban residential area, Crato.

ITINERARY III *Idanha: Border Country*

Alter do Chão

Monastery of Flor da Rosa, Crato.

Despite successive periods of rebuilding, the walls and turrets that surround the town of Crato still display signs of the building techniques typically used in the Islamic period. The layout of the streets in the historical centre is similarly traditional in its design.

C. T.

Leave Crato by Estrada Nacional No. 245 and go towards Alter do Chão, roughly 12 km. away.

III.9 **ALTER DO CHÃO** (option)

III.9.a Castle

Open: 10.00-12.30 and 14.00-17.30 (April-October); in other months, all visits must be booked two days in advance at the Information Office: tel: 245 61 00 04.

This small fortification was profoundly remodelled in the 14th century and its earlier history is generally ignored by written sources. The castle's semicircular corner towers, surmounted by conical pinnacles, are extremely eye catching and were clearly built at a later date. The base of these towers is, however, much older and displays typical features of the building systems normally associated with the Emirates period. With the nearby ruins of Alter Pedroso and Cabeço de Vide, this whole area provides suggestive evidence of an important settlement from the earliest days of Islamicisation. Roughly 4 km. away, it is possible to visit the Coudelarias de Alter (Royal Stud), where a breed of horses descending from ancient Andalusian lineage is still bred and maintained.

C. T.

Natural Park of São Mamede
In the vast plain of the Alentejo with its gentle, undulating horizons, there suddenly and unexpectedly rises up a rocky outcrop 1025 m. high and formed from various mountain ranges, amongst which the most important is the Serra de São Mamede. Schists, greywackes, limestones and quartzites mingle together in a colourful miscellany of extremely beautiful morphological configurations, which contrast with the granite of the plains, resulting in the enormous variety of soil. The Park of Serra de São Mamede spreads over an area of 31,750 hectares in the municipalities of Arronches, Castelo de Vide, Marvão and Portalegre. Because of the combination of altitude and a lithology with varying climatic conditions, it contains a wide range of different species of flora and fauna. In view of both the quantity and variety of bird species nesting

Idanha: Border Country
Alter do Chao

Castle, Alter do Chao.

here, one of the most striking features about this nature reserve is its birds, a huge variety of which nest here. They include such species as the Bonelli's eagle, the griffon vulture, the short-toed eagle, the round-winged eagle, the black stork and nocturnal species such as the eagle owl and wood-owl. Previously under threat of extinction, the communities of indigenous deer and wild boar are slowly beginning to return to their natural habitats. The green valleys of the Serra de São Mamede have long attracted human settlement, so that it is not surprising to find here the ruins of the Roman city of Alamia, the ancient bridge at Portagem and the mediaeval castles of Marvão and Vide. Agriculture is the quintessential economic activity of these diverse villages, splashing white specks across the hillsides with their typical Mediterranean appearance. To the North, the landscape is divided into separate compartments, alternating oak-groves and groves of wild chestnuts with olive-trees, pine-trees and eucalyptus, dryland pastures with irrigated land, whilst in the South the predominant feature is the extensive plains full of cork-oaks and holm-oaks, amidst which the cattle graze peacefully.
One event that should not be missed by visitors to the Natural Park of São Mamede is the Chestnut Fair in Marvão. Equally unforgettable are the interesting regional handicrafts, in particular the cork products, tapestry and the manufacture of textile fibres.

C. G./P. N.

Information Centre: Praceta Heróis da Índia, 8-1°, 7300 Portalegre.

Badajoz and Mérida (Spain)
Passing over the border at Caia and crossing over the River Guadiana, one enters the modern suburbs that surround the old Islamic City of Badajoz. Inside some monumental dry-mud walls built in the Almohad period, is a modern archaeological museum with an important Islamic collection.

ITINERARY IV

The Road to the Gharb

Cláudio Torres, Santiago Macias, Fernando Branco Correia,
Artur Goulart de Melo Borges

IV.1 ELVAS
        IV.1.a Entrance to the Citadel
        IV.1.b Porta do Templo

IV.2 JUROMENHA (option)
        IV.2.a Fortifications

IV.3 ALANDROAL (option)
        IV.3.a Castle

IV.4 VILA VIÇOSA (option)
        IV.4.a Castle

IV.5 ÉVORA
        IV.5.a Islamic Évora
        IV.5.b Évora Museum
        IV.5.c Évora City Walls

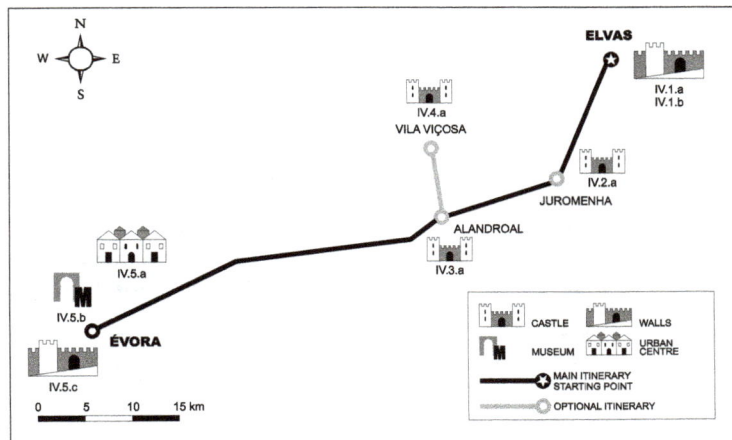

Castle, horseshoe arc, Alandroal.

ITINERARY IV *The Road to the Gharb*

Alandroal, detail, 16th century drawing, in Duarte d'Armas, "Livro das Fortalezas".

The Alto Alentejo continues to be one of the least studied and least known territories of Gharb al-Andalus. Only now, for instance, are we beginning to suspect the importance enjoyed by places such as Veiros in Islamic times. Other places, for example, Cabeço de Vide and Monforte, are still in the early stages of research, although they are known to have been fortified settlements. Besides Juromenha, which is mentioned in the texts of geographers and historians, there are other places, such as Avis, Estremoz or Montemor-o-Novo, where there were areas of between two and four hectares that were definitely quite heavily populated. There is, for example, a tombstone (from a fairly late period) carved out of marble from Estremoz, which was possibly removed from the Alentejo to São Tomé de Aguião (Arcos de Valdevez), from where it was taken to the National Archaeological Museum in 1905. In other cases, given the absence of archaeological data, it is possible to hazard more architectural and functional interpretations of certain places. The most interesting and enigmatic case is undoubtedly that of Portel Castle. Besides the actual place name, naturally referring to the existence of a dry port, the imposing bulk of the feudal castle was violently superimposed onto an older settlement, which had some turrets and sections of wall that are still visible here and there inside the old walled area. To the north of the River Tagus, the process of Islamicisation took place along the south-north axis of the Roman road linking Lisbon to Santarém, Coimbra and Braga. The Alto Alentejo, on the other hand, was organised around an intersection of this same road, which extended on to Beja and Mértola, with another road that marked out the essential structure of the region between the coast and the strongholds of the Iberian plateau. This east-west route had as its most important points the cities of Qasr Abudanis (Alcácer do Sal), Évora and Mérida. The foundation of Badajoz, taking place at the height of the period of the emirs and under the protection of the Banu Marwan family, strengthened the logic of this axis, which thereafter incorporated the fertile region of the upper Guadiana Valley. Cities of particular note in this territory were the old and decadent Mérida, Badajoz (with an area of 10 hectares contained within its walls), which became the capital of the Aftasid Dynasty in the $5^{th}/11^{th}$ century. The urban centres of Elvas, Évora and Alcácer, with an area of seven hectares contained within its walls were also important. This was a large territory with concentrated settlements, which was crossed by an intense traffic in trade between the continental inland region and the ports of the Rivers Sado and Tagus.

C. T. / S. M.

ITINERARY IV   *The Road to the Gharb*
Elvas

IV.I ELVAS

*Information: Praça da República,
tel: 268 62 22 36.*

The existence of Elvas as a settlement in Islamic times is clearly documented in Islamic sources from the 4th/10th century, but it may have existed well before this. Two linear remains of what were the walls, forming part of the Islamic defensive system at Elvas, testify to the impressive size of this urban centre, described by the geographer al-Idrisi in the 12th century as a *medina* or "city". Whilst this author was not indifferent to the beauty of the women that he encountered here, other 5th/11th century writers were pleasantly surprised by the richness of the countryside surrounding Elvas. This information is clearly reflected in the many different marks left on the region's toponymy. At an urban level (with names such as Alcamim, Alcalá and Almocovar), and at a rural level (with names such as Torre do Mouro (the Moor's tower), Seixo dos Mouros (Moors' rock), Herdade do Mouro (the Moor's estate), Horta do Mouro (the Moor's orchard), Vale do Mouro (the Moor's Valley), or even Fonte (fountain) de Axá, Poço (well) de Almourim, Alcarapinha, Alpedrede, Alfarófia, etc.).

Elvas underwent a major building programme under the period of Almohad rule, with works that inevitably transformed the citadel (see Porta do Templo) and the wall of the *medina*. This wall enclosing an area of roughly 10 hectares still retains some evidence of the original dry-mud wall built around most of its perimeter for defensive purposes, and it was further strengthened with L-shaped gateways (which have since disappeared). Amongst today's remains of the fortifications, attention is drawn to a partly altered polygonal tower, known nowadays as the Arco da Encarnação.

Both in the citadel and the ancient *medina*, the urban layout still consists today of narrow winding streets that evoke memories of an Islamic heritage of several centuries. The Islamic presence in Elvas did not cease when the city was brought under the control of the Portuguese crown. In the 15th century, the community of "*mouros forros*" (emancipated Moors) or Mudejars was the second most important of its kind in the whole of the Alentejo. The Moors of Elvas made a living as craftsmen, whilst also mastering the technology required for tending their crops and maintaining close trading links with the neighbouring kingdom.

Elvas must also be included in the list of Portuguese places where the epigraphy of Islamic times has clearly left its mark.

Entrance to the Citadel, Elvas.

ITINERARY IV   *The Road to the Gharb*
Elvas

In fact, although foundation stones incised with Arabic characters, which until at least the 17th century were still to be found in the walls of the *medina*, have since disappeared a tombstone was recently found in a place that has not been identified with great exactitude. Judging by the type of calligraphy used, however, it probably dates from the mid-6th/12th century.

F. B. C.

IV.1.a Entrance to the Citadel

The so-called Porta da Alcáçova (Citadel Gate) or Arco do Miradeiro (Watchtower Arch) has the form of a right-angled passageway, flanked by two sturdy quadrangular towers. Large granite blocks were used in its construction, probably originating from an earlier Roman construction, if not in fact from an ancient Roman or late Roman defensive system.

Although the entrance arch is nowadays more or less semicircular in shape, this gate previously had a surmounted or horseshoe arch, which was destroyed in 1887. Fortunately, there remained a stereotype of the original entrance made by a Polish citizen who had visited Elvas earlier. Apparently, it was an arch without any frame or *alfiz*. This set of circumstances suggests that there was an entrance system which, in chronological terms, may correspond to the periods of the emirs and *caliphs* (3rd/9th - 4th/10th centuries).

F. B. C.

IV.1.b Porta do Templo

Largo de Santa Clara.

In the Christian period, this gateway leading inside the citadel came to be known as the Porta do Templo (Temple Gate), as this was where the regional headquarters of the religious and military order of the Knights Templar was located.
Today, in order to enter the space of the Islamic citadel, one has to pass through an archway that has been opened directly into the surrounding *tabiyya* (dry-mud) wall. Earlier, for defensive reasons, access was much more complicated, and the gateway had a 90-degree bend in it.
This gateway has since become part of a private house, although it is still visible from the street. It is an L-shaped double entrance with an intermediate chamber or courtyard. A partially reconstructed gateway can be seen defined by a horseshoe arch, which, unlike the Arco do Miradeiro, has an outer frame or *alfiz*.

Porta do Templo, Elvas.

ITINERARY IV *The Road to the Gharb*
Juromenha

Fortification, Juromenha.

In structural and typological terms, this entrance was built at a later stage than the Arco do Miradeiro and is very probably the result of expansion work carried out during the period of Almohad rule, because of its obvious parallels with similar defensive systems dating from this time.

F. B. C.

Leave Elvas by Estrada Nacional No. 4, heading towards Spain, and turn right at the crossroads along Estrada Nacional No. 373. Roughly 17 km. further on, turn left to Juromenha.

IV.2 **JUROMENHA** (option)

IV.2.a Fortifications

Visits must be booked in advance through the Junta de Freguesia (Parish Council), tel: 268 96 90 02.

The Juromenha fortifications, protected by the Ribeira de Mures and the River Guadiana and controlling one of its natural harbours, were built in an area of fertile land and rivers that are full of fish. There are also several remains of ancient mining structures to be found in the surrounding area. The fortifications occupy a dominant position, from where it is possible to see as far as Badajoz in the distance.

Although the building of the fortifications, which began in the 17th century, was to destroy much of the evidence of earlier occupations on the site, a large part of the mediaeval perimeter wall still remains, and most notably the sections dating from the Islamic period.

At the north-east end, there still stands a solid masonry tower, in which three stones have been placed dating from the Visigothic period (two of them taken

ITINERARY IV The Road to the Gharb
Alandroal

Castle, Alandroal.

from a frieze, whilst the other originates from the base of an altar). This tower may belong to the period when most of the western territory of the Iberian Peninsula attempted to assert its autonomy in relation to the power of Cordoba, under the leadership of Abd al-Rahman Ibn Marwan al-Jilliqi, in the $3^{rd}/9^{th}$ century. Built against this tower are sections of a drymud wall of the military type. These walls, whose last period of rebuilding must have taken place in the Almohad period, present a set of regular-shaped towers placed immediately next to the above-mentioned tower. These towers have very little space between them and no L-shaped entrances, so that they are similar to the fortifications typically built in the period of the *Caliphs* ($4^{th}/10^{th}$ century).
Islamic geographers from the $4^{th}/10^{th}$ century in fact, mention Juromenha. Ibn Sahib al-Sala provides abundant detail about its occupation by Geraldo Sem Pavor and his men, during the years from 561/1166 to 564/1169. According to the philosopher Ibn Arabi, writing at the end of the $6^{th}/12^{th}$ and beginning of the $7^{th}/13^{th}$ century, it functioned as a *ribat*, or fortified Muslim hermitage, dedicated to the *jihad*.
Archaeological excavations carried out in the fortifications revealed a set of silos used for the storage of grain, which must first have been used in Islamic times.

F. B. C.

Return to Estrada Nacional No. 373 and head towards Alandroal (roughly 16 km.).

IV.3 **ALANDROAL** (option)

IV.3.a **Castle**

Information: Rua de Olivença, tel: 268 44 00 40.

Alandroal Castle stands as a clear demonstration of the powerful influence exerted by the "emancipated Moors" or Mudejars who remained in this region, even after the incorporation of this territory into the Portuguese kingdom.

ITINERARY IV   *The Road to the Gharb*
Vila Viçosa

Castle, narrow path, Alandroal.

It is a fortification that was commissioned at the end of the 13th century by the Order of Avis, more precisely in 1298, during the reign of D. Dinis.
Its architect, mason, or master builder was the Muslim Master Calvo. Remarkably, he was not prevented by the Lords of the town and castle from inserting a corner stone in the tower, to the right of one of the castle's gateways, which identifies him as the author of the building work. Furthermore he uses an expression that is equivalent to the motto of the Nasrid kings of Granada. However, the evidence of his predilection for Islamic features does not end there, as a number of aspects relating to the castle's construction demonstrate. For instance, his preference for quadrangular towers and the existence of other inscriptions that are to be found in the walls denote a clear Islamic influence. Note also the small window with a horseshoe arch, framed by an *alfiz*, a feature that was commonly found in the decorative systems of the final phase of Islamic rule.
Because of this particular set of circumstances, Alandroal Castle is one of the finest examples of Mudejar art in the Alentejo, with all that this implied of the compromise between the dominant mediaeval Christian world and an Islamic minority that still clung to its own values and forms.

F. B. C.

Leave Alandroal by Estrada Nacional No. 255 in the direction of Vila Viçosa. For Évora, follow Estrada Nacional No. 373 as far as the crossroads leading to Redondo and then turn onto Estrada Nacional No. 254 leading to Évora.

IV.4 **VILA VIÇOSA**

IV.4.a **Castle**

Information: Praça da República, tel: 268 88 11 01. Entrance fee. Open: 9.00-13.00 and 15.00-18.00 (Tuesdays to Sundays); closed on Mondays and public holidays.

Little now remains of an old wall that once surrounded the Islamic settlement here.

ITINERARY IV *The Road to the Gharb*
Évora

Castle, Vila Viçosa.

After its conquest by the Christians, the town took the name of Vila Viçosa and was granted a charter in 1270. The present-day defensive system dates largely from the 14th century. A major part of the old urban complex was destroyed at the beginning of the 16th century in order to build a solid fort with ramparts, which was completed in 1537. Inside the beautiful Renaissance fortress of the Dukes of Bragança, there is a significant collection of archaeological artefacts, including some remarkable ceramic objects from the Islamic period that were found inside the settlement.

C. T.

For Évora, take Estrada Nacional No. 254, in the direction of Redondo.

IV.5 ÉVORA

IV.5.a **Islamic Évora**

Information: Praça do Giraldo, tel: 266 70 26 71.

Although the city never enjoyed the same importance as other large urban centres in al-Andalus, the remains that are left of the Islamic period are more than enough to justify taking a closer look.
Even the city walls, rebuilt at the end of 3rd-b. 4th/b. 10th century and enclosing an area of seven hectares, were attributed for many years to the Romans or Visigoths. They are, however, closely linked to one of the most famous episodes in the history of Islamic Évora.
According to a report by Ibn Hajjan, on the night of 19 August 300/913, the armies of Ordonho II "entered the city, where the fighting and slaughter reached a state of paroxysm, with many perishing on both sides, until the Christians imposed themselves in number, defeating them and causing them to seek refuge in the eastern part of the city". Only a few inhabitants who had taken refuge at the top of some old buildings managed to escape towards Beja in the dead of night. After this disaster "all the people of the West

ITINERARY IV *The Road to the Gharb*
Évora

were most disturbed [...] and began to repair their walls, protect their weak points and diligently strengthen their ramparts". Ibn Hajjan's 5th/11th-century report in *Muqtabis* V is corroborated by the epigraph that is still preserved today at Évora Museum and which alludes to the building work (302/915).

It is known that the citadel was located in the area now occupied by the Palace of the Counts of Basto and that the cathedral was built on the site of the congregational mosque.

Whilst a careful re-reading of the existing documents and close study of the city walls has made it possible to revise a number of ideas about Islamic Évora, it must also be stressed that there are a number of other features from this period scattered around the city. The *caliphal* capitals that discreetly decorate two windows of the Palace of the Dukes of Cadaval, for example, and there are also some inscriptions either celebrating buildings that were commissioned in the city or marking the death of faithful worshippers at various times.

S. M. / C. T.

IV.5.b **Évora Museum**

Largo Conde de Vila Flor, tel: 266 70 26 04. Entrance fee, except on Sunday mornings. Open: 9.30-12.30 and 14.00-17.30; closed on Mondays and Tuesday mornings.

The Museum's Islamic section was formed from several disparate finds and collections. These include the archaeological collection of the archbishop of Évora, D. Frei Manuel do Cenáculo (1802-1814), pieces that had been found in the city and were stored at the Public Library, a number of acquisitions and donations, and several pieces unearthed during recent excavations at the museum building itself. Although the section includes sculpture, ceramics and coins, perhaps the most representative group of exhibits consists of the stone epigraphs, five of which come from Évora and one from Mértola, originating from Cenáculo's collection.

Walls, partial view, Évora.

ITINERARY IV   The Road to the Gharb

Évora

Marble Capital, e. 4th/10th century, Évora Museum.

Stone Tablet with commemorative inscriptions, 302/915, Évora Museum.

Of particular interest is the oldest stone that has so far been found on Portuguese territory. The stone is inscribed in Arabic and the writing is in relief, in an archaic *kufic* script, and it can be dated back to 302/915, since it refers to the reconstruction of Évora. According to clearly established historical data, this was the date when the city was rebuilt by the Lord of Badajoz, after it had been abandoned one year before, as a result of the invasion and bloody pillaging that it suffered at the hands of Ordonho II of Galicia. This marble fragment has the peculiarity of having been re-used roughly two centuries later. For on the other side is an inscription commemorating the construction of a building commissioned by the then Lord of Évora and an important figure in the period of the second *Taifa* kingdoms, Abu Muhammad Sidray Ibn Wazir al-Qaysi.
Equally noteworthy are two late 6th/11th-century lintels with epigraphs inscribed upon them and a 7th/13th-century tombstone with a "symbolic" arch and profuse decoration. Of the three 4th/10th-century capitals contained in the collection, two are recent acquisitions and were originally found at Beja in the 1940s during remodelling work on a building. They are identical in both their manufacture and size and are two excellent and well-preserved examples testifying to the refinement of the art of sculpture at the end of the period of the *Caliph*s.
The archaeological work which was carried out inside the museum to look at the possibility of enlarging the already existing cellar, revealed a series of structures and materials essential to improving our knowledge of the Islamic period in Évora. The finds resulting from this exploration represent the first such residential unit that has been unearthed in the city. It was also possible to identify another older level, from the Emirs' period, as well as a more extensive group of buildings from a much later period (5th/11th century). Amongst these, of special note, is a latrine and its corresponding ditch, which is in a good state of preservation.
The objects that were found here, particularly the ceramic pieces made in the *cuerda seca* technique and those glazed with manganese and green, have greatly enriched the collection, helping to contextualise it in historical and museographical terms in Islamic Évora.

A. G. M. B.

ITINERARY IV The Road to the Gharb
Évora

IV.5.c **Évora City Walls**

In a city dominated by the Roman Temple of Diana and so full of memories of the Roman period and the Renaissance, it is, inevitably, very difficult for the Islamic period to achieve great visibility. Taking advantage of earlier building materials and imitating the Roman design in a somewhat irregular fashion, Évora's Islamic Wall (built at the end of 3rd-b. 4th/b. 10th century) introduced traditional architectural features from Syria into the western region of the Iberian Peninsula. Now, however, to mark a difference, there was a shorter distance between each of the turrets and these in turn did not project so far from the wall itself. All that remains of the walls where Ibn Abdun or Ibn Wazir once passed and that once surrounded the city, are two short but quite expressive sections. One section to the north of the city (that stands opposite Évora University and on which the Palace

of the Counts of Basto was built), and another to the west (inside a building, at No. 5 Rua de Burgos, housing a department of the Ministry of Culture).

S. M.

Palace of the Counts of Basto, section of wall, Évora.

*We suggest continuing with the MWNF Spanish Exhibition **Mudejar Art: Islamic Aesthetics in Christan Art**, and exploring Itinerary X, Nobility and Monastic Patronage, which includes the cities of Guadalupe, Llerena, Zafra and Calera de León.*

Rua de Burgos, section of wall, Évora.

103

ITINERARY V

A Taifa Kingdom: Mértola

Santiago Macias, Cláudio Torres, Miguel Rego, Maria João Vieira

V.1 BEJA
    V.1.a Islamic Beja
    V.1.b Queen Leonor Museum

V.2 MOURA
    V.2.a Castle
    V.2.b Moura Roman Museum
    V.2.c Moorish Quarter and Arab Well

V.2 NOUDAR
    V.3.a Castle

V.4 SERPA-THE WHITE TOWN
    V.4.a Historical Town
    V.4.b Town Walls
    V.4.c Serpa Archaeological Museum

V.5 MÉRTOLA
    V.5.a Mértola Museum
    V.5.b Islamic Quarter
    V.5.c Castle
    V.5.d Parish Church of Nossa Senhora da Anunciação (a former mosque)

Weaving Workshops

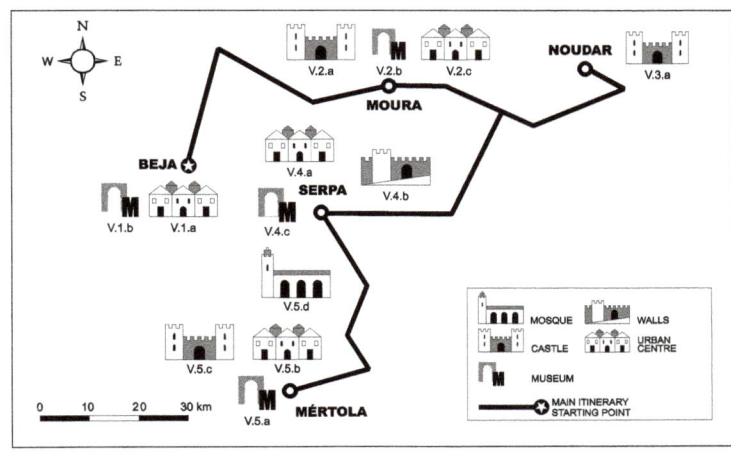

Parish Church (former mosque), interior, Mértola.

ITINERARY V   A Taifa Kingdom: Mértola

Mértola.

This itinerary is largely confined to the ancient district of Beja, a vast area stretching from the Atlantic coast to the Serra de Aracena (a range of mountains that now belongs to the Spanish province of Huelva) and organised around a road that connected the cities of Beja and Mértola. In fact, a whole region was organised around this road, stretching from the left bank of the River Guadiana (where Aroche was the main town, followed by Moura, Serpa, Noudar and Totalica (Santo Aleixo) as far as the upper valley of the River Sado or the Ribeira de São Romão. Closer to the coast, but in a less inhabited area, was the fortified hill of Santiago do Cacém, standing above an old lagoon and the Port of Sines, whose name in the Islamic period was Marsa Hasine.

Further south, in the mountain hollows, were the fortified settlements of Castro da Cola, Ourique and Odemira and the *burj* (tower) of Mesas do Castelinho. These places belonged to a district that stretched as far as the desert-like cliffs of the West Coast. A scattered population of shepherds and smallholders, whose history has been a long story of survival, seems to have controlled these fortified points.

The history of this region in the Islamic period matched what was happening in the main seats of power. For more than five centuries (from 92/711 to 647/1250), this vast territory was the setting for a permanent struggle between the centralising pull of Cordoba and Seville, and attempts by the local population to establish their own autonomy.

ITINERARY V   A Taifa Kingdom: Mértola

It is in this same context that the rebellions of Beja (f. h. 2nd/mid-8th century) should be viewed, and likewise the successive rebellions which followed. Those led by the Banu Marwan family (mid-3rd/s. h. 9th century), the *Taifa* kingdoms in the mid-5th/11th century and the military campaigns fuelled by Ibn Qasi in the mid-6th/12th century.

In addition to the region's strong agricultural traditions, justifying a dense population of *villae* in the Roman period, the Baixo Alentejo's reputation as an important source of different metals lasted well into the Islamic period.

The ancient poets described how the sun would set in the West, as it plunged into torrents of liquid gold and brought an ardent glow to the day's end. The gold and metal-bearing wealth of Iberia was, however, much stronger than the myth. We now know that for many centuries the most inhospitable mountainous regions of the Baixo Alentejo contained rich seams of various ore.

Ibn Razi mentioned that in the Islamic period there existed in the region of Beja an important mine of pure silver. Known then as Totalica and nowadays identified with the village of Santo Aleixo (Moura), it was said that "the settlers have concealed it and make use thereof", or, in other words, that the place where the local inhabitants mined the ore was kept a closely guarded secret. Copper continued to be mined in Islamic times, being extracted in small quantities from the old Roman mines

107

in the copper-bearing seams of the Alentejo, although the archaeological evidence of this activity is rather scanty. At that time, bronze continued to be the main raw material used in the production of metal objects for everyday domestic purposes, ranging from buckles, spindle heads and earrings to harnesses and other fittings for weapons and coats of armour.

Written documentation about the Islamic period in the Beja region is particularly scarce, so that most of what has in fact been written about this period is based on archaeological evidence, topographical interpretations, or information sometimes provided by the region's place names. According to Ibn Ghalib "the *cora* (district) of Beja borders on that of Mérida. Its land favours the cultivation of cereals and the rearing of cattle. Its flowers are good for the bees and there is therefore much honey. Its waters have the property of tanning hides in an incomparable manner. Its territory is enormous and contains fortresses, cities and districts. Amongst its cities are Alcácer do Sal and Aroche. The journey from Beja to Mérida takes three days on horseback". It is, however, difficult in the present context to identify the sort of landscape that would have existed in the Islamic period. The successive efforts made to clear the land, particularly those that took place during the 19th century, have given the region its present-day appearance, which is certainly very different from that which would have unfolded before the eyes of the Gharb's inhabitants some 1000 years ago. In terms of the region's architectural history, very few Islamic structures have survived in a recognisable state. The past is hidden behind successive alterations and expansions that have taken place through time, such as the walls built in the feudal period, the ramparts dating from the time of the Restoration, and the rapid urban growth of the 19th century.

From the physical viewpoint, most of the places themselves are also difficult to recognise, even taking into account the archaeological work undertaken recently. In many places, the Islamic occupation is only confirmed by the presence of the occasional feature remaining from that period. Sometimes it is only the place names, its topography or the actual logic of the land's occupation that make it possible to identify the importance of certain places in Islamic times. In some cases, such as that of Aljustrel for instance, little has remained from the physical point of view, whilst in other cases, such as in Ourique, time and humankind have taken it

Container, 6th/12th-7th/13th century, Queen Leonor Museum, Beja.

ITINERARY V   A Taifa Kingdom: Mértola
Beja

upon themselves to eliminate most of what was left of the Islamic past.
This catalogue has omitted some of the rural sites or other places that, because of their isolation, are difficult to include as part of the Itinerary. This group includes archaeological sites of undeniable interest, such as Alcaria Longa or Mesas do Castelinho.
Different fates were to befall some of the region's main urban centres. Beja recovered much of its former glory after the "Reconquest", once again becoming the region's key city. Century after century, it was to acquire greater importance and power, as part of a process of expansion that nowadays makes it difficult for us to identify the remains of the Islamic past in the heart of the modern-day city.
Mértola, however, proved to be a completely different case altogether. A prolonged period of stagnation throughout the mediaeval and modern ages has meant that some of its remains from the Islamic period have survived until the present day in a recognisable state. This is the case, for example, with a section of the northern wall, and, in particular, with some of the architectural features of the city's former mosque.
Other places of lesser importance during the period, such as Moura, Serpa, Noudar or Aroche, have not only retained their respective castles – where sections of Almohad walls are sometimes clearly visible – but also display other archaeological remains and in some cases have even kept alive some enthralling legends. S. M. / C. T.

V.1 **BEJA**

V.1.a Islamic Beja

Information: Rua Capitão João Francisco de Sousa, 25, tel: 284 31 19 13.

Bowl decorated in green and Manganese, $4^{th}/10^{th}$ century, Mértola Museum.

Having enjoyed a brilliant past in Roman and mediaeval times, Beja frequently played an important role in the political evolution of Gharb al-Andalus. On several occasions, the city was the centre of important rebellions against the political hegemony of the large urban centres, such as Cordoba and Seville.
According to al-Maqqari, the territory of Beja not only possessed a large number of silver mines, but also had the "glory of being the birthplace of al-Mutamid Ibn Abad". Another author al-Razi, in the *General Chronicle of Spain* in 1344, stated: "Beja is one of the oldest cities in Spain and was built at the time of Julius Caesar, who was the first of the Caesars. And Julius was the first to begin to mark out and divide the land into plots. Beja is a very good and arable land, excellent for the rearing of cattle. And it is a very good land for hives, for there are very good flowers, most excellent for bees. And the water of Beja is naturally good for the tanning of leather. And the city has many good wide streets".

ITINERARY V   A Taifa Kingdom: Mértola

Beja

Tombstone of Marble, 487/1095, Queen Leonor Museum, Beja.

Beja's *Mozarab* community is said to have enjoyed a certain amount of power. This is suggested by the persistence of ancient forms of Christian worship and the work that was undertaken at the Igreja de Santo Amaro, rebuilt or modified in the 4th/10th-5th/11th century.

Marble Tombstone, 531/1136, Queen Leonor Museum, Beja.

From the 5th/11th century onwards, with the increasing importance of Évora and mainly with the territory's political division into the *Taifa* kingdoms, Beja entered upon a period of sharp decline, so that it is not surprising that the heavily fortified city of Mértola should sporadically have become the regional capital.

Today, the successive building programmes undertaken in the historical centre have hidden most of the remains of the Islamic City. The most important of these works were certainly those that took place in the 19th century, when extensive areas of the mediaeval city were demolished. The late Islamic horseshoe arch of the castle keep, some epigraphs at the Regional Museum and the odd ceramic piece are the only visible remains of what was once one of the most important cities in Gharb al-Andalus.

S. M.

V.1.b Queen Leonor Museum

Largo da Conceição, entrance to the museum through the church of the Convento da Conceição, tel: 284 32 33 51.
Entrance fee. Open: 9.30-12.30 and 14.00-17.15; closed on Mondays and public holidays.

The first archaeological collection in Beja was that put together by D. Frei Manuel do Cenáculo Villas-Boas at the end of the 18th century. When he was promoted to Archbishop of Évora in 1802, part of the palace's archaeological collection was transferred to Évora.
The Archaeological Museum of Beja was only inaugurated in 1892, largely due to the dedication and commitment of José Umbelino Palma, with the museum's collection

consisting of essentially Roman materials found in the city of Beja, which at that time was undergoing extensive rebuilding work. In 1927-28, the Beja Regional Museum was installed in the section that still remained from the Mosteiro de Nossa Senhora da Conceição, which is currently the home of its central collection.

In a building that is most heavily marked by the memory of the great passion of Sister Mariana Alcoforado for a French chevalier, there are not many pieces to be found from the Islamic period. In the Museum's catalogue compiled in the 1950s, only two tombstones from this period are mentioned. Since then, some more items (in particular those originating from Castro da Cola) have been incorporated into the museum's collection, although it still cannot be said that the existing pieces really do justice to Beja's importance as an Islamic city. The Beja Regional Museum has an important and expressive collection of epigraphs, consisting mainly of tombstones, quite probably originating from the city's Moorish cemetery or cemeteries. A collection of beautifully calligraphed tablets were brought here from the former Jesuit college, although these are not normally exhibited to the public and are believed to have belonged to D. Frei Manuel do Cenáculo. The museum has six tombstones, four of which are dated. The oldest of these epigraphs dates from 440/1048-479/1087 and marks the death of Malik Ibn Hassan. The most recent of these stones from Beja is dated 531/1136 and refers to a certain Muhammad Ibn Mufarrish Ibn Hud. Leite de Vasconcelos first makes mention of it, and it is a tombstone from the early Christian period, which was later re-used on the other side for the Arabic inscription. It formed part of the foundations of the new dormitory of the Convento da Conceição and was included in the museum's collection after building work was carried out there in May 1896. The Convento da Conceição has been classified as a National Monument since 1922.

S. M.

Leave Beja by the IP2, heading in the direction of Évora. Roughly 21 km. further on, turn onto Estrada Nacional No. 258 towards Moura.

V.2 MOURA

V.2.a **Castle**

Information: Largo de Santa Clara, tel: 285 25 13 75.

Castle, tower set in mud wall, Moura.

ITINERARY V   A Taifa Kingdom: Mértola

Moura

Castle, commemorative stone tablet in celebration of the construction for the mosque's minaret, 444/1052, Moura.

Moura Castle is closely bound up with the Romantic legend of the Moorish Maiden, Saluquia, said to be the daughter of the city's last *alcaide*. In fact the word "celoquia" refers to a tower, and popular tradition has simply given it another significance.
A small settlement in the Islamic period, its walls encircled an area of two hectares. Some fragments of the Almohad perimeter wall (mid-6th/12th century) have survived, although this was mostly destroyed in the second half of the century. Of the dry-mud walls that once surrounded this, there still remains as the most important section a quadrangular turret situated above the building that now houses the Municipal Library. Ever since some relatively recent restoration work was undertaken, it is rather more difficult to make out the whitewash that previously imitated large masonry blocks on its main façade, one which is similar to that on the castles of Alcácer do Sal or Salir (Loulé). Moura Castle has been classified as a Building of Public Interest since 1944.

S. M.

V.2.b Moura Roman Museum

Rua da Romeira, tel: 285 25 00 40.
Open: May to September: Tuesday-Friday: 9.30-12.30 and 14.30-18.00; Saturdays and Sundays: 10.00-12.30 and 16.00-19.00; October to April: Tuesdays-Fridays: 9.30-12.30 and 14.30-18.00; Saturdays and Sundays: 10.00-12.30 and 14.30-17.00; closed on Mondays.

This small Municipal Museum holds a number of exhibits that testify to the town's Islamic past.
Besides the ceramics from the *Caliph* period, this collection also contains two painted bone panels that belonged to a small chest possibly made in a workshop in Granada in the 7th/13th century. A traceried rosette in the centre, which is flanked by two human figures, dominates the decorative system. Plant bulbs with long stems and lotus flowers suggest a paradisiacal atmosphere.
Also worthy of mention are the rare tombstones, and in particular the one dating from 769/1368, or, in other words, more than 130 years after the town's reconquest. Having been discovered by chance in the same area, they have made it possible to locate the town's Moorish cemetery, which was situated next to what is now referred to as the Mouraria (Moorish Quarter).
In the area around the castle's fountain, attention is drawn to a plaque commemorating the building of the mosque's minaret, commissioned by al-Mutadid in the mid-5th/11th century (probable date: 444/1052).

S. M.

V.2.c Moorish Quarter and Arab Well

To visit the Arab well, contact Sra. Joaquina Rosa Silva, 2ª Rua da Mouraria, nº 28, tel: 285 25 13 77.

ITINERARY V *A Taifa Kingdom: Mértola*
Noudar

After the town's "Reconquest" in 629/ 1232, the more affluent families emigrated to the kingdom of Granada, the last refuge of Islam in the Iberian Peninsula. Those who stayed were subjected to the new rulers and went to live in a residential quarter built to the west of the castle. Although partially destroyed by the building of new walls in the 17th century and somewhat adulterated by less felicitous architectural alterations made over the years, the Moorish Quarter has been classified as a Building of Public Interest since 1993. Today it consists of three streets, an alley and a small square, whilst the typical urban features of a mediaeval quarter are well preserved.
In the Largo da Mouraria (Town Square), an old house can be visited that contains the mouth of a 14th-century well.

S. M.

Rua da Mouraria, Arabic well, 8th / 14th century, Moura.

On leaving Moura, take Estrada Nacional No. 258, heading in the direction of Spain. At Barrancos, turn towards Noudar.

The Legend of the Moorish Maiden, Saluquia
There is a most romantic legend, probably created in the 19th century, which tells of the tragic story of the wedding day on which the Moorish Maiden, Saluquia, from Moura, was due to marry Prince Brafama from the neighbouring town of Aroche.
Brafama, the Lord of Aroche, was on his way to Moura to marry Saluquia, when Christian horsemen ambushed him. Having defeated and killed the Moors, the Christians donned their clothes and continued on to Moura, pretending to be the wedding party.
Saluquia ordered the gates to be opened, but realising that she had been tricked threw herself from the castle walls with the keys to the fortress in her hand.
The legend has been perpetuated in the town's coat of arms, which depict Saluquia lying at the foot of the tower.

S. M.

V.3 **NOUDAR**

V.3.a **Castle**

Information: Câmara Municipal de Barrancos, tel: 285 95 06 30.
Open: 08.00-19.00; closed on Mondays.

At the start of Islamic presence in the Iberian Peninsula, Noudar, which was situated at the limits of the *cora* of Beja,

Noudar

Castle, Noudar.

Slate Tombstone, 473/1080, Noudar.

would have been little more than a small settlement. Towards the end of the 4th/10th and the beginning of the 5th/11th century, it strengthened its defences by building a humble *hisn* or *burj* made of dried mud. Some remains of this wall are still visible in the area around the castle's citadel, although largely concealed by the schist wall built in the 14th century.

Overlooking the road that connected the region of Beja and Moura to the old "Silver Route" through Jerez de los Caballeros, the castle served as a watchtower. This function was suggested by its location and by the synonym of the place's actual name (the Arabic word *nadara* means "to see" or "to watch"). The fortified structure stood at the highest point of an extensive rocky outcrop between the Múrtega and Ardila Rivers, where previously there had been a small early Christian basilica, whilst the residential quarter spread around the whole of the hillside except the southern slope.

Several artefacts that originate from here suggest the strategic importance of the area. For instance, the two tombstones bearing Arabic writing, a collection of 5th/11th-century silver coins, a tip of a dagger sheath and a large collection of 7th/13th-century ceramics. Evidently this was an important site in a territory that borders on the district of Badajoz, whose uninterrupted occupation only came to an end in the mid-19th century.

Conquered in the first half of the 7th/13th century, Noudar was given to the Order of Avis, which built the present-day walled fortress with an enclosed area of roughly 12,000 sq. m. The town received a charter in 1295 from D. Dinis and in 1308 it became the first refuge for fugitives in Portugal.

M. R.

ITINERARY V   A Taifa Kingdom: Mértola
Noudar

Castle, Noudar.

The archaelogical items mentioned in the text are currently undergoing restoration for their future exhibition to the public.

For Serpa, return to Estrada Nacional No. 258 as far as Moura and then take Estrada Nacional No. 255 leading to Pias / Serpa (roughly 76 km.).

Natural Park of Aroche Peak and Aracena Sierra (Spain)
The plains gradually blend into the western slopes of the Serra Morena. The extensive tablelands of the Beja region funnel into the valleys etched out by the Chança, Múrtega and Ardila Rivers. The Aracena Sierra and the Aroche Peak rise up to the east and, through their physical presence, impose the political frontier of the Cora of Beja. In the $4^{th}/10^{th}$ and $5^{th}/11^{th}$ centuries Further eastwards, in the district of al-Munastir (Almonaster la Real), the gateway to the Abbadid Kingdom of Seville defended the roads leading to the mining region of Andévalo and the capital itself on the banks of the River Guadalquivir. According to al-Razi in the $4^{th}/10^{th}$ century, between this territory and that ruled by the Aftasid expansionists of Badajoz Arun (Aroche), there was a castle that belonged to the Beja district.

Because of its topographic features, the region that today forms the Aracena Sierra and the Aroche Peak played an important role in marking the boundaries between the region's three main centres of attraction: Beja and Mértola, Badajoz and Seville. The mountains were but sparsely populated. Most of the inhabitants lived in small groups of scattered huts, although these were sometimes in sufficient number to be enclosed within simple walls to defend the cattle and residents, as at Aracena, or encircled by fortified walls of a military nature, as at Cortegana. The mountains formed a region that was rich in chestnut, holm-oak and cork-oak trees and was also ideal for cattle rearing, the production of honey and the tanning of animal skins. Therefore the area never ceased being a highly coveted territory in periods when the warring factions of the regional political powers caused serious divisions.

M. R.

Almonaster, Aroche and Señora de la Peña (Spain)
At the highest point of Al-Munastir, a castle

ITINERARY V   A Taifa Kingdom: Mértola
Serpa-The White Town

was built with an area of roughly 8,000 sq. m. To the north lies Almonaster la Real, a town whose main period of growth began in the 15th century. The walled mediaeval structure was built on the remains of walls from the Roman period and, inside the citadel, the Islamic mosque was converted into a chapel dedicated to Nuestra Señora de la Concepción.

The mosque was built using the remains of Roman and early Christian structures and its mihrab and qibla wall, that date from the 2nd/8th-3rd/9th centuries, are considered to be amongst the oldest surviving examples in Western Islam.

Al-Munastir was the seat of the military and fiscal district in the 4th/10th century, facing towards the territory of Beja / Mértola of which Awrus / Aroche was the easternmost fortress.

The 6th/12th-7th/13th-century wall in the present-day castle of Aroche is still preserved, and as little as 500 m. to the north east, the remains of a residential suburb were recently found, very probably abandoned at the end of the 5th/11th century.

The militarisation of settlements located at key points in the territory of Beja / Mértola began in the 5th/11th century. This process necessitated walls to be built around Alfajar or Alfayat de la Peña, 2 km. from La Puebla de Guzmán, one of the castles conquered by the army of D. Sancho II in 636/1239, during his incursion from Mértola to Tavira. Today, all that is still to be seen of Alfajar is the area where the fortress once stood, the remains of its thick walls and some of its houses. Nearby their now stands the shrine of the Virgen de la Peña.

M. R.

V.4 SERPA-THE WHITE TOWN

V.4.a **Historical Town**

Information: Largo D. Jorge de Melo, 2-3, tel: 284 54 47 27.

Serpa is one of those towns where one can sense the continuity of human occupation, its long evolution over the centuries, marked by the coexistence and superimposition of successive historical settlements.

The town's past still remains somewhat unclear so that only fresh archaeological finds in the urban area can help to provide more

Urban residential area, Serpa.

ITINERARY V   *A Taifa Kingdom: Mértola*
Serpa-The White Town

precise information. Although the intense use made of the town's spaces and the juxtaposition of everyday activities make it difficult to interpret the original urban fabric two main centres of activity can be identified.

At one end of the town, at its highest point, is the Old Castle, as it has come to be known popularly, marking the oldest perimeter of the settlement. It was there that the first houses appeared, protected by a castle and its walls, and where there is now a small residential quarter of low houses and narrow winding streets. Indifferent to its neighbouring lay-buildings, the Parish Church of Santa Maria, believed to be a consecrated former mosque, stands proudly.

At the other end of the town, the walls built by D. Dinis formed an enclosure that became the town's residential and administrative centre from the 14th-15th centuries onwards.

Although there is little doubt that cities reflect complex forms of social organisation, it is nonetheless commonplace to speak of the aristocratic features of the town of Serpa. With its many examples of erudite architecture and its noble houses proudly displaying their family crests, Serpa is also extremely rich aesthetically, in terms of the decorative air given to the walls of its "poor" inhabitants' houses. It is after all, this town's whitewashed houses that make it so full of light.

M. J. V.

V.4.b Town Walls

To visit the walls, you should start at the Tourist Office and climb the steps leading to the Church of Santa Maria, or you can enter the town through the Porta Nova (New Gate) and walk through the so-called Bairro do Castelo Velho (Old Castle District).
Open: 9.00-12.30 and 14.00-17.30.

Castle, Serpa.

Walls, Serpa.

ITINERARY V   A Taifa Kingdom: Mértola
Serpa-The White Town

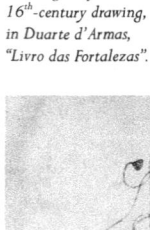

Castle of Serpa, 16th-century drawing, in Duarte d'Armas, "Livro das Fortalezas".

Located roughly 5 km. from the River Guadiana, Serpa was an important fortified settlement overlooking fertile farming land just before the Christian Reconquest. The old wall, built at the top of a small hill, was strategically positioned and enclosed an area of 21,000 sq. m.

At the end of the 13th century, D. Dinis made an effort to reorganise the Alentejo along Christian lines, granting the town its second charter, that of Évora / Ávila. Then in this border town where conflicts were a frequent event, he built an imposing wall enclosing an area of 68,000 sq. m.

The *Crónica* of Rui de Pina tells us that the monarch "almost completely rebuilt all the towns of the upper Odiana, namely Serpa, Moura, Olivença, Campo Maior and Ouguela, whose fortresses he founded at great expense".

This same chronicler, writing at the turn of the 15th to the 16th century, but who was also inspired by earlier documents, does not deny that a Muslim town existed here which was later re-founded by D. Dinis, where he ordered the castle to be built from scratch.

Evidence of the town's Islamic past can still be seen in some sections of the *tabiyya* wall and two towers (Torre da Horta and Torre do Relógio), which were partially reused in the building of the Christian castle.

It is also quite possible that the bell tower of the Santa Maria Church, which houses a cylindrical structure on its inside, is living testimony of the minaret which once belonged to the town's former mosque.

M. J. V.

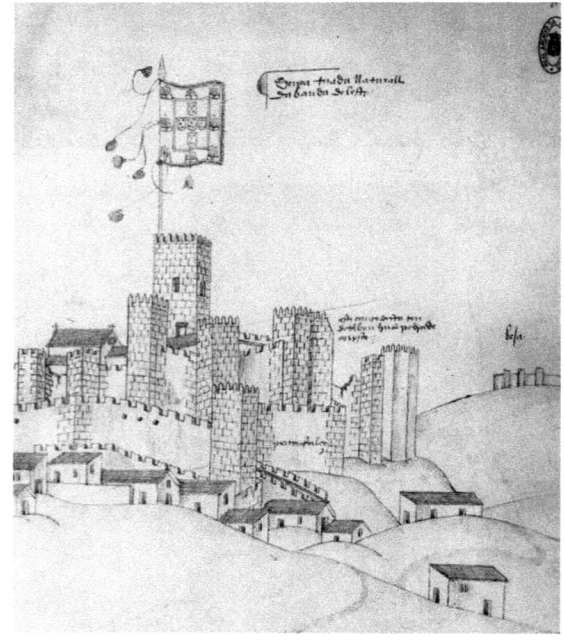

V.4.c Serpa Archaeological Museum

Alcáçova do Castelo, tel: 284) 54 01 00.
Open: 9.00-12.30 and 14.00-17.30.

The 1980s were a particularly fruitful decade for the creation and renewal of local municipal museums in Portugal. The Serpa Archaeological Museum came into being in 1982.

The museum is located inside the citadel of the old castle, in the former governor's residence, which was later transformed into a prison. It has a small collection of Islamic exhibits, mostly originating from Cidade das Rosas, an important Roman villa which was still inhabited in the Islamic period. These remains (fragments of pottery and metal artefacts) were found mostly amidst a pile of ashes and burnt earth, which lay on top of some Visigothic lime kilns. These in

turn showed signs of having re-used structures of the former Roman baths.
Amongst the objects on display, one of the most remarkable is a bowl dating from the period of the *Caliphs* and a knife with a bone handle, which is believed to date from the same period. The most famous exhibit, however, is a small slab of slate with an inscription in *kufic* – the reproduction of a verse from the *Qur'an* – on one side, and four crescents of different sizes on the other. This is a mould that was used to manufacture amulets from molten metal, intended for individual use. It was found in the area close to the Roman villa of Zambujeiro, near Pias.

M. J. V.

Head towards Spain and turn right at the crossroads leading to Mértola, following Estrada Nacional No. 265 (roughly 50 km.).

V.5 MÉRTOLA

Information: Largo Vasco da Gama, tel: 286 61 25 73.

"And Mértola lies on the banks of the River Odiana; and it is a very old castle and has some old buildings". The literature of the period can tell us little more than this reference by al-Razi about Mértola in Islamic times. We do, however, know that the city was far more important than such scanty information would suggest.
Taking full advantage of its exceptional positioning on a rocky outcrop between the Guadiana and one of its tributaries, the ancient city of Mértola was already famous amongst geographers of ancient times for the imposing nature of its fortifications.
Mértola covered an area of roughly 60,000 sq. m. and had a population of no more than 2,000. In its golden period, the city would undoubtedly have had more inhabitants if the existence of at least two outlying residential districts were considered. One in the area beyond the river (Além-Rio) and the other at the entrance gate of the Porta de Beja, close to an early Christian chapel that was later dedicated to Santo António dos Pescadores (Saint Anthony of the Fishermen).
The streets of the present-day city run parallel to the river and are interconnected by narrow passageways, certainly they make use of the earlier urban layout of the Islamic period. However, despite the fact that the walls, constantly repaired over time, still respect their original mediaeval

Slate Mould of amulet, 6th/12th-7th/13th centuries, Serpa Archaeological Museum.

ITINERARY V   A Taifa Kingdom: Mértola
Mértola

General View, Mértola.

design, occasionally only can it be attributed to the Islamic period. All that can be recognised of the Almohad period, for example, is the northern perimeter wall with its massive quadrangular towers.

Amongst the exuberance of the city's Roman and Christian remains, and after two decades of archaeological studies, significant features have now been found from the Islamic period that clearly justify the importance enjoyed by the city until its conquest by the Knights of the Order of Santiago in 635/1238.

In addition to the walls, the basic layout of which has remained unaltered since the Roman period, and which still retains small sections dating from Islamic times, the most important data is almost certainly provided by the remains of the former mosque. Also significant were the excavations of an extensive residential district built in the $6^{th}/12^{th}$ century, on which part of the archaeological work has been centred.

S. M.

V.5.a Mértola Museum

Largo da Misericórdia.
Date of opening: 2001.
Entrance fee. Open: 9.00-12.30 and 14.00-17.30.

Two decades of archaeological work has made it possible to put together the most important collection yet of materials from the Islamic period in Portugal and has also led to an endless string of questions about the life of the various local populations during the period.

ITINERARY V   A Taifa Kingdom: Mértola

Mértola

Set of containers, Mértola Museum.

More than anything else, it is the everyday life of Islamic Mértola that can be sensed in most of the pieces exhibited at this museum. Looking at these pieces, the visitor cannot help but think of the uses to which they were put, who used them, how and when. Research undertaken by archaeologists, anthropologists and ceramologists have made it possible to create a set of functional groups for the use of ceramics. Whilst, in the past, it was only possible to see undifferentiated artefacts (or more prosaically shards of different pots), we can now identify cooking utensils, storage pots, luxurious tableware and sophisticated pitchers and water-pots.

The meeting of roads and the intermingling of people that the city of Mértola encouraged in the past are clearly demonstrated by the diversity of pieces put together in the collection. In the exhibition there are also a variety of luxurious pots imported from the Tunisian region (and probably made in Tunis or Kairouan), as well as others produced at workshops in Seville and Almería or even by modest craftsmen from the southern region of the Gharb. It is true to say that the most significant part of this collection consists of ceramics, and that those that have been best preserved have successfully withstood most unfavourable conditions. There are also some interesting pieces of jewellery, glassware and other artefacts that have so far proved difficult to situate amongst the details of everyday life.

The bowl depicting a hunting scene is one of the most beautiful and rare pieces in the Mértola Museum. By employing a technique using green and manganese decorations a hunting scene is depicted in which a greyhound and falcon simultaneously attack a gazelle. Most skilfully drawn and coloured, this bowl is part of a set of several pieces, each with an identical shape and form and using the same technique to create a decorative style which is to be found scattered around various places in the Western Mediterranean region (Denia, Majorca, Pisa and Kairouan). Although the origin of this bowl is believed to be Tunisia, recent research does not exclude the pos-

Bowl with hunting scenery, $5^{th}/11^{th}$ century, Mértola Museum.

ITINERARY V   A Taifa Kingdom: Mértola

Mértola

Islamic Quarter, excavations, Mértola.

Castle, Tower of the Homage, Mértola.

tours may be booked through the Tourist Office, tel: 286 61 25 73.

In the mid-6th/12th century a group of houses were built on the remains of the abandoned Roman palace but they stood only a very short time. Abandoned after the Christian Conquest of Mértola, this Islamic Quarter was only to see the light of day again in the course of the excavations currently being carried out there. Roughly 15 houses may be identified, and excavations may soon uncover another similar number. With minor variations, these houses repeat the architectural patterns that were established by the Graeco-Roman civilisation and spread throughout the whole of the Mediterranean urban world. There was a central courtyard around which a series of different rooms (alcoves, kitchens and latrines) were organised with clearly defined functions. Excavations have revealed the remains of masonry and dry-mud walls, fragments of lime, floors made of brick or mortar and concave roof-tiles which perfectly identify the Mediterranean cultural environment to which these houses belonged.
In the complex superimposition of structures that always results from archaeological investigations of urban sites, it is still possible to identify clearly the remains of streets and drainage systems that bear testimony to the last occupation of the Islamic citadel.

S. M.

sibility of the bowl being produced in the Iberian Peninsula.

S. M.

V.5.b Islamic Quarter

Access to the Quarter is by Rua do Cemitério. Open: Monday-Friday: 9.00-12.30 and 14.00-17.30; closed at weekends, but guided

V.5.c Castle

The fortification that was built at the behest of the Knights of the Order of Santiago at the end of the 13th century was superimposed on earlier constructions dating back to the Iron Age and the Roman and Islamic periods. Over many centuries, roman soldiers, the likes of Ibn Qasi (the Lord of Mértola in the

ITINERARY V   *A Taifa Kingdom: Mértola*
Mértola

mid-6th/12th century), traders, artisans and warriors had all passed through the sites where the keep and walls from the Christian period now stand. Successive restoration and rebuilding work has meant that few features from the time of the *Caliphs* are still visible. A closer analysis does, however, reveal the imposts of a horseshoe arch at the entrance gate and the presence of an Islamic cistern in the centre of the castle. Close to this cistern, recent excavations have unearthed part of a residential quarter, abandoned at the end of 6th/f. h. 12th century.
S. M.

V.5.d. **Parish Church of Nossa Senhora da Anunciação (a former mosque)**

Largo da Igreja. Guided tours must be booked through the Tourist Office, tel: 286 61 25 73. Open: 10.00-12.00 and 14.15-17.00.

The Mértola mosque was built in the mid-6th/12th century on a site previously occupied by another religious building. The structure of Mértola's Congregational Mosque remained largely unaltered until the beginning of the 16th century, when it was drawn by Duarte d'Armas, who refers to it as the "church which was once a mosque". This precious drawing depicts a temple with five naves (each of which has a pitched roof) and it is also possible to recognise the minaret, which the Christian Lords had adapted to form a bell-tower. The building's progressive degradation led to major repair work being undertaken in the first half of the 16th century. Financed by D. João de Mascarenhas and carried out around 1530, these building works were to significantly alter the building's volumetry. In particular, the

Parish Church of Nossa Senhora de Anunciação (former mosque), Mértola.

123

ITINERARY V A Taifa Kingdom: Mértola

Mértola

Mosque, door, Mértola.

After these successive alterations and restoration work, what now remains of the Mértola Mosque are the outer walls and four small doors (three of them opening onto the former courtyard and one leading to the outside) where the slightly stilted horseshoe arch is framed by an *alfiz*. Inside the church it is possible to identify the polygonal *mihrab*, which still contains its stuccoed decoration, but now without the polychrome effects. There are three multi-lobed blind arches, above it, a cornice framed by two cordons, expressing the idea of infinity, a theme that is repeated at the top of the moulding.
Even though the exoticism of its interior may be misleading, the rest of the building reflects the building work undertaken in the 16th century or even later.
Mértola's present-day Parish Church has been classified as a National Monument since 1910.

S. M.

Mosque, mihrab, Mértola.

roof was vaulted, which meant increasing the height of the walls and building powerful buttresses.

Natural Park of Vale do Guadiana
Covering an area of 70,000 hectares, this natural park stretches along the banks of the River Guadiana through the municipalities of Mértola and Serpa. The Ribeira de Limas to the Ribeira de Vascão marks the southern border of the Alentejo. Here, amidst vast expanses of holm-oak and cork-oak groves, it is possible to see great birds, such as the bustard and the bittern, hovering above the open plains. Long rugged valleys still conserve their dense Mediterranean woodland, which provides a natural habitat for a variety of wildlife. Deep in the park, the River Guadiana squeezes between the steep slopes of narrow gorges, where on occasion the water gushes forth in turbulent waterfalls.

C. T.

WEAVING WORKSHOPS

Santiago Macías

Open: Monday-Friday: 9.00-12.30 and 14.00-18.00. Although closed at weekends, guided tours may be arranged through the Tourist Office, tel: 286 61 25 73.

For hundreds of years, the women of this region have worked at home weaving the blankets that their families use to protect themselves against the cold winter nights. Shearing, washing, carding, spinning, weaving ... an endlessly repeated cycle that has continued into the 21st century as a final echo of the rural lifestyle of the southern Alentejo.

Until recently faced with the threat of extinction, the slow work of reviving this activity involved the study and identification of patterns, the organisation of vocational training courses and the gradual recommencement of a profession that was thought to be redundant. Over the years, the Mértola Weaving Cooperative has been the repository of knowledge on this craft and has taken it upon itself to promote the activity through the exhibition and sale of its products.

We suggest continuing with the MWNF Spanish Exhibition **Mudejar Art: Islamic Aesthetics in Christan Art**, *and exploring Itinerary X,* Nobility and Monastic Patronage, *which includes the cities of Guadalupe, Llerena, Zafra and Calera de León.*

Woman working
in the textile factory,
Mértola.

ITINERARY VI

Guadiana: The Great Southern River

Santiago Macias, Cláudio Torres, Cristina Garcia, Paula Noronha

VI.1 ALCOUTIM
　　　VI.1.a Old Castle

VI.2 CASTRO MARIM (option)
　　　VI.2.a Castle

VI.3 CACELA VELHA (option)
　　　VI.3.a Historic Village

VI.4 TAVIRA
　　　VI.4.a Ruins of the Citadel at Tavira Castle
　　　VI.4.b Tavira Vase

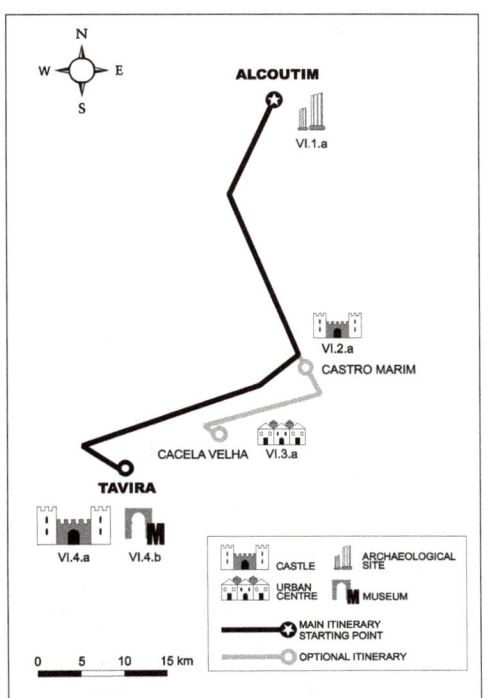

Castro Marim.

For the Mediterranean sailors who made their way westwards, the passage between the Pillars of Hercules (the Strait of Gibraltar as seen in the atlas) represented the beginning of what was the final trade route. Beyond this point there were still a few other ports that were worth visiting: Cádiz, Faro, Silves and, for those prepared to venture upriver, Mértola.

From the mouth of the Guadiana to the cliffs of Sagres, there stretched a tranquil coastline, visited since pre-Roman times by merchants and sailors with a frequency that continued under the dominion of Rome and into the Islamic period.

From the point of view of its monuments, the eastern region of the Algarve is not the most important area in Gharb al-Andalus. Similarly, from the historical point of view, the territories to be found here were usually referred to in a somewhat off hand manner, being considered of minor importance in a region where the cities of Faro and Silves represented powerful centres of attraction.

This eastern area of the Algarve was, and still is, marked by the profound contrasts to be found between a range of mountains whose archaic settlements were to remain largely unchanged almost until the present day, and a coastal region that has always been open to cosmopolitan influences. The Serra do Caldeirão still bears evidence of some cylindrical shaped houses built with a masonry base and topped with a conical roof thatched with straw or broom. Today, these houses are used for haystacks or as barns and are to be found scattered throughout the Algarvian uplands as far as the present-day municipalities of Mértola and Almodôvar in the Alentejo.

In the remote inland regions, various archaeological projects have been regularly undertaken over recent years.

Amongst a series of excavations in a number of small villages perhaps the most important, particularly in terms of size, are those at Cerro das Relíquias, close to the Ribeira de Vascão, and the old Castle of Alcoutim overlooking the River Guadiana. Because of difficulties with access, we only recommend visiting the latter.

To the south of Alcoutim, the River Guadiana passes through such places as Montinho das Laranjeiras, Guerreiros do Rio and Odeleite. Some of these places are located upon sites that date back to Roman times, where life remained largely unchanged until the $5^{th}/11^{th}$ century. On these small alluvium platforms, the Roman *villae* survived well into the Middle Ages and were subjected to a gradual process of Islamicisation, as demonstrated by archaeological discoveries, without, however, ever losing contact with the major Mediterranean trade routes. In addition to this series of Roman *villae*, all along the river there were a number of fortified settlements dating from pre-Roman times, which remained active well into the Islamic period.

In the marshland of the Guadiana valley, a prominent feature was the small rocky outcrop upon which stood the Castle of Castro Marim. There is documentary evidence to support the notion that the area was occupied by Punic, Roman and Islamic settlers. The surrounding region cannot, however, have enjoyed great prosperity. To judge by the poverty of the remains from the Islamic period found at places such as Vale do Boto, this region of salt marshes was inhabited by fishermen and salters who were certainly not endowed with great resources. Tavira, as an urban centre, and Cacela, its sentinel, standing at the entrance to the river, were the most important places in this territory. However, even if only the Algarve region is taken into con-

Castle, Castro Marim.

sideration, neither place played a particularly major role. From what can be discovered of Tavira, looking at the region it occupied and the written sources available, the region enjoyed some importance at the end of the Islamic period. The results of archaeological work currently in progress to assess the importance of Cacela are still awaited. Curiously, the pieces that have been gathered there are now stored at the National Archaeological Museum in Lisbon, which underlines the importance of Cacela in more remote times.

The most heavily populated areas were those around the City of Tavira, where the existence of many allotments and orchards, now gradually disappearing amidst modern urban developments, indicates that the region has long enjoyed sophisticated irrigation systems.

Even taking into account the tradition of piracy surrounding Islamic Tavira, it is nonetheless clear that the comments made by the geographer al-Idrisi ($6^{th}/12^{th}$ century) about the area of Ceuta can also be applied to this coastline where there has always been an abundance of fish. "Close on one hundred different species can be counted, with the local inhabitants dedicating themselves in particular to the catching of the large fish known as tuna, which is found in great numbers in this region. It is caught with harpoons fitted at the end with projecting hooks that penetrate into the fish's body and do not then come out. The wood of the harpoon is protected by long cords of hemp that are wound around it. These fishermen are so well practised at their art and so skilful that they are without any known rivals anywhere else in the world."

S. M.

ITINERARY VI *Guadiana: The Great Southern River*
Alcoutim

The Old Castle, Alcoutim.

VI.1 ALCOUTIM

VI.1.a Old Castle

The castle is roughly 1.5 km. from the town at Cerro de Santa Bárbara.
Information: Praça da República, tel: 281 54 61 79.

Roughly 1 km. to the north of Alcoutim, the old castle stands atop a small hill in a strategic position overlooking the River Guadiana. The surrounding area, which has not yet been completely studied, contains an important group of rural mining settlements from Islamic times, which suggest that they were to some extent dependent on the castle itself.

The fortifications were probably built in the $3^{rd}/9^{th}$ century, since, according to archaeological data, this is the date of the castle walls (enclosing an area of little more than 700 sq. m.), as well as the cistern and the buildings that marked the first phase of settlement. The area was inhabited until the period of the *Taifa* Kingdoms in the mid-$5^{th}/11^{th}$ century, and the old castle of Alcoutim was abandoned at the end of this century, with there being no evidence of its being inhabited during the Almoravid and Almohad periods.

S. M.

On leaving Alcoutim, follow Estrada Nacional No. 122-1 and after roughly 6 km., turn left onto Estrada Nacional No. 122, heading in the direction of Castro Marim / Vila Real de Santo António.

VI.2 CASTRO MARIM (option)

VI.2.a Castle

Information: Praça 1° de Maio, 2, tel: 281 53 12 32.
Open: Monday-Friday: 9.00-17.30.

Close to the mouth of the River Guadiana and facing the fortified city of Ayamonte across the border, Castro Marim was a small, fortified settlement in the Islamic period, acting as a sea port and trading centre.
For many years, the site was incorrectly identified as being the Marsa Hasin that is mentioned in Arabic sources, although the remains discovered from the pre-Roman period lead us to believe that the place may have enjoyed some prominence at the begin-

ITINERARY VI   *Guadiana: The Great Southern River*
Cacela Velha

Castle, Castro Marim.

ning of the process of Islamicisation. Amongst ruined fortifications from different periods, it is possible that the so-called Old Castle – a square-shaped enclosed area reinforced at the corners with semi-cylindrical towers – corresponds to, or was built upon, an earlier fortress whose architectural roots can be traced back to Byzantine military traditions from the Emirate period.

C. T.

After travelling 6 km. in the direction of Faro, turn right at the crossroads and head in the same direction along Estrada Nacional No. 125. At the 12 Km. sign, turn left towards Cacela Velha (roughly 13 km.).

For Tavira, continue along Estrada Nacional No. 125 until you reach the respective crossroads.

VI.3 **CACELA VELHA** (option)

VI.3.a **Historic Village**

For anyone visiting Cacela Velha nowadays, the most visible reminder of its historical past is the church and, above all, the bulwarks of the village's 17th-century fortifications. All that remains from the Islamic period is a small section of the *tabiyya* wall in the south east. However, both the small village and the region around it played an important role during the Islamic period. This is confirmed both by archaeological data gathered in the immediate surroundings and the fact that this was the birthplace of the poet Ibn Darraj al-Qastalli, one of the most important literary figures in al-Andalus.

Fortress, Cacela Velha.

ITINERARY VI   *Guadiana: The Great Southern River*
Cacela Velha

Cacela Velha.

Due to the fact that it controlled the entrance to the River Gilão, Cacela was clearly very closely linked to Tavira during the Islamic period. More important than this, however, evidently it was the fertile land between the two places that justified the unusually high quantity of archaeological finds there. Quite apart from the tombstone of the Mozarab Bishop Julião (d.349/961) a number of other artefacts have been found in this area. Two bronze lamps were discovered (one belonging to the collection of the National Archaeological Museum, whilst the whereabouts of the other is not known), as well as the ablutions font mentioned earlier in this guide that today forms part of the same museum's collection.

Regardless of the undeniably valuable results expected from the archaeological work currently in progress, Cacela's interest for visitors is borne out not only by the wealth of its Islamic past but also by the unusual beauty of the area in which the museum is located.

S. M.

For Tavira, return to Estrada Nacional No. 125 and head in the direction of Faro / Tavira (roughly 7.5 km.).

Bridge over the River Gilão, Tavira.

ITINERARY VI   *Guadiana: The Great Southern River*
Tavira

Octagonal Tower, Tavira.

VI.4 **TAVIRA**

Information: Rua da Galeria, 9, tel: 281 32 25 11.

Even today, Tavira remains as one of the most beautiful cities in the Algarve, although in Islamic times, its settlement would have been restricted to the small hill on the right bank of the River Gilão. From the walls built in this period, all that now remains are some cubic turrets and the odd fragment of the perimeter wall, which is not always easily identifiable.

In a city whose valuable heritage is largely symbolised by its bridge and pyramid-like roofs, there are a number of features to be seen still from the Islamic period. From the topographical point of view, it seems clear that the town mentioned by al-Idrisi and Yaqut as being a village, would have been somewhat more than that. The five-acre area, rebuilt in Christian times, testifies to a period of economic power that has since been confirmed by recent archaeological discoveries.

Nowadays, it is difficult to identify Islamic Tavira, particularly at its highest points, since both time and human settlements have inevitably caused a number of alterations. On the site where a small citadel once stood, a garden has now been planted, whilst the former mosque has since been replaced by the Church of Santa Maria do Castelo.

Close to the river, not far from where the town hall now stands, there once would have been the city port, where both fishermen and traders would have lived in quarters built downstream from the bridge and alongside the sandy beaches where their boats would have been moored.

S. M.

133

ITINERARY VI   *Guadiana: The Great Southern River*

Tavira

Section of wall, Tavira.

VI.4.a Ruins of the Citadel at Tavira Castle

Open: Mondays: 9.00-17.30, Tuesday-Friday: 8.30-17.30, Saturdays, Sundays and public holidays 10.00-19.30 (summer) and 9.00-17.30 (winter).

For many years, the replacement of old abandoned citadels by either gardens or cemeteries was common practice. Tavira was no exception to this rule. Next to the Church of Santa Maria do Castelo (probably a former mosque) are some sections of wall, which are difficult to date and now provide the backdrop for a small garden. The memory of the city's mediaeval fortifications is kept alive by an octagonal tower that has been rebuilt on various occasions and which hypothetically stands on the base of an earlier construction from the Almohad period.

S. M.

VI.4.b The Tavira Vase

Recent archaeological work undertaken by Manuel and Maria Maia has led to the discovery of various materials that can be dated back to the $5^{th}/11^{th}$ century. Particularly impressive are various red-clay pieces, which are painted with a clear *engobe* (a slip consisting of a mixture of white clay and water). Mention should also be made here of a clay vase surmounted by an extraordinary group of human figures and animals, modelled in keeping with the popular taste. Some of the zoomorphic motifs would have served to pour water or some other liquid into the container. Three knights, two men, one woman and a series of animals would seem to suggest the ritualisation of a wedding dance.

S. M. / C. T.

This piece will be on display to the public from 2000 onwards. For more information, contact the Tourist Office: Rua da Galeria, 9, tel: 281 32 25 11.

ITINERARY VI   *Guadiana: The Great Southern River*
Tavira

Natural Park of Ria Formosa
The Algarve's Natural Park of Ria Formosa is distinguished by its five islands and two sandy peninsulas preventing the force of the sea from disturbing a peaceful lagoon of canals interlaced with salt marshes and tiny islands, cyclically bathed by the tidal waters. Having been formally recognised by the Convention of Ramsar, the Ria Formosa is the temporary home to migratory birds from northern and central Europe, some of which stop off on their way to the African continent. Thus, from October to March, thousands of birds nest and feed in the dunes, salt pans and marshland. It is possible to observe many species of birds here, such as the little tern, white heron, flamingo, kingfisher, avocet, ringed plover, European stilt and the moorhen, the symbol of the nature reserve. This discreet expanse of marshland, with its strange vegetation, either submerged or laid bare by the ebb and flow of the tides is rich in wildlife and plant life. Together with the extreme mobility of the chain of dunes, similarly full of botanical species of great interest, it represents one of the most productive and vulnerable systems known to man.
The local populations are linked to the lagoon by intense economic activity. This is not only through fishing, the gathering of shellfish and mollusc culture, salt production and pisciculture, but also because the park serves as a reserve or nursery for different species of fish, including the gilthead, bass and sea-bream. Not to be missed on a visit to the Natural Park of Ria Formosa are the guided treks organised by the Marim Centre of Environmental Education, as well as the chance to enjoy a boat trip on the Ria Formosa or to sample the local gastronomic specialities.

C. G. / P. N.

Information Centre: Centro de Educação Ambiental de Marim, 8700 Olhão, tel: 289 70 41 34/5.

The Tavira Vase, 5th / 11th century.

Niebla
After crossing the Guadiana to Ayamonte, you need only travel a few dozen km. before you reach the banks of the Rio Tinto where the ancient city of Niebla still stands. On several occasions this city was the capital of a vast kingdom that, in its latter stages, included the territory of the Algarve. The whole area of the original settlement, measuring 10 hectares, is completely enclosed by one of the most beautiful walls still remaining in the former al-Andalus. Dry mud is the only material used in its construction and only the corners of the towers and gates make use of blocks of marble or granite. Inside the town, we highly recommend a visit to the old Church of Santa Maria, where the basic structures of an Almohad Mosque were recently brought to light. Its minaret, which is still intact, continues to be used as a bell-tower.

C. T.

ITINERARY VII

Between the Algarve and the Mountains

Santiago Macias

VII.1 FARO
　　VII.1.a Faro Archaeological Museum
　　VII.1.b Town Gate
　　VII.1.c Arco do Repouso

VII.2 LOULÉ
　　VII.2.a Islamic Loulé
　　VII.2.b Loulé Museum

VII.3 VILAMOURA
　　VII.3.a Ruins of Cerro da Vila

VII.4 SALIR
　　VII.4.a Fortified Settlement

VII.5 CASTRO DA COLA (option)
　　VII.5.a Excavated Ruins of the Fort

VII.6 PADERNE
　　VII.6.a Castle

VII.7 ALBUFEIRA
　　VII.7.a Albufeira Archaeological Museum

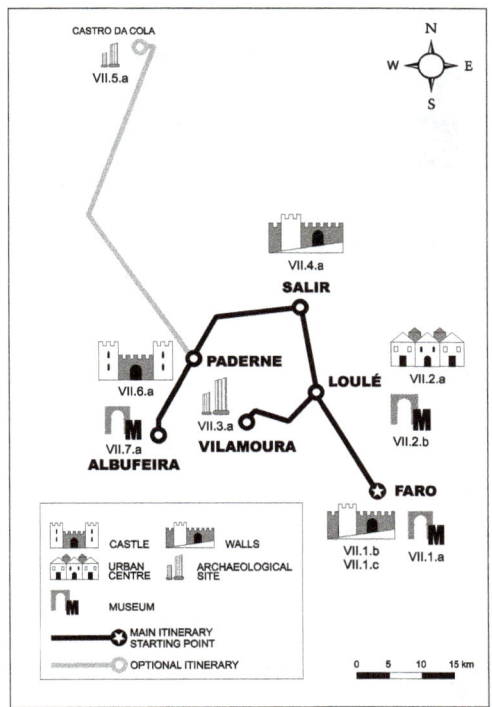

Castle, Paderne.

ITINERARY VII   *Between the Algarve and the Mountains*

Castle, Paderne.

The history of the region of Faro in the Islamic period is marked by two circumstances: the first is the unusual richness of its territory, the second is the importance that the Mozarab Christian community continued to enjoy, without ever weakening, throughout the whole period of the spread of Islam.

The first of these two factors is amply borne out by the evidence contained in the reports of the geographers of that period. Al-Razi, al-Himyari or al-Idrisi, all are very clear about this particular aspect. The first of these authors wrote in the mid-$4^{th}/10^{th}$ century: "… And Ossónoba … lies on very good and very flat land; and has many good trees and very good crops. And within its boundaries there are very good mountains where many animals might be reared. And it is a land of many streams. And it is very good hunting land, both in the hills and in the rivers. And nearby the sea can be seen stretching forth into the distance. And there are many good and very pleasant islets where boats can land. And there are very good and very well irrigated orchards with very good and very pure fruits. And within its boundaries there are many pine trees. Its benefits make it one of the best places in the world. And there is very good amber in the river of Ossónoba."

According to another author, al-Bakri, a form of tin was mined in this area that was unrivalled for its similarity with silver.

On the other hand, the fertility of the orchards and gardens made this region one of the most heavily populated in Gharb al-Andalus. Roman *villae* such as Milreu or Cerro da Vila (Vilamoura) were not abandoned, and continued to supply the urban markets, remaining inhabited until the $5^{th}/11^{th}$ century.

The region's history, together with the continuing presence of the Mozarab community, are other factors that lend some support to the theory of civilisational continuity. Despite the region's dependence on Seville, a local family (the Banu Bakr Clan) controlled the region in the $3^{rd}/9^{th}$ century. The complete silence about the Algarve until the first *fitna* and the regular fashion in which governors who remained obedient to Cordoba followed on from one another can only be seen as representing an atmosphere of peace in a territory where life was to continue unchanged without any great disturbances. Only at the end of the $3^{rd}/9^{th}$ century was there once again mention of the region of Faro and, even so, within the context of the autonomy of the Algarve itself. It was around this time that Bakr Ibn Yahya Ibn

Bakr, a *muwallad* (a member of an indigenous family that had converted to Islam) took control of the city of Faro. He founded a dynasty and also seized control of a territory that stretched as far as Silves and the western coast. The chronicler Ibn Idhari said: "He established himself in Santa Maria, erected buildings and transformed the city into a powerful castle that he then equipped with iron gates. The city had a system of administration, weapons, good soldiers and abundant provisions [...]. One was able to travel within his territory with the greatest possible safety". Whether or not they had converted to the Islamic faith, traditional families from the region seem to have maintained their power to control economic and political affairs entirely intact. During the period of the *Taifa* Kingdoms in the $5^{th}/11^{th}$ century, their importance was once again evident: between 416/1026 and 444/1053, it was the Banu Harun family, who was also *muwallad*, who controlled the territory. During the course of this century, in place of the old name of Ossónoba, the city began to be known as Santa Maria and had a magnificent church, with columns that legend said were made of silver. Thereafter, the city's Mozarab name was used more and more, although it was the word *harun* (certainly derived from an ancient lighthouse – farol in Portuguese – in the vicinity) that ended up giving its name to the city.

Over the last three decades, particularly, the Algarve coast has undergone a profound process of change. These changes have not only increasingly hidden the face of the Islamic past in the cities but also destroyed old irrigation systems and irreversibly changed the typically southern European social and productive structures that had remained almost completely unaltered throughout the Middle and Modern Ages.

Even so, in the region of Faro, it is possible to identify a large number of places of interest displaying signs of the Islamic past. In addition to the main city, where recent expansions have made it very difficult to see the mediaeval nucleus, Loulé, which, with a walled area of five hectares, was the region's second largest centre of population, is worth some attention. In the area known as the Barrocal, the more barren limestone region of the Algarve, two of the most notable places were Paderne (Albufeira) and Salir (Loulé), with their *tabiyya* fortifications from the Almohad period. Near the coast, excavations and restoration work has revealed a Roman site at Cerro da Vila (Vilamoura), where archaeological investigations have also been directed towards studying the Islamic occupation of the site.

In addition to the places that are included in this Itinerary, there are many others whose place names or simple traditions denote that they were places of some importance in Islamic times. The most sig-

Wall, Salir.

ITINERARY VII *Between the Algarve and the Mountains*
Faro

Arco do Repouso, Faro.

nificant example is the tourist town of Albufeira (literally meaning "the lake"), whose name points to the existence of a harbour, protected in the past by a peninsula. Today it is difficult to envisage the topography of mediaeval Albufeira amongst the various modern urban developments. The small cove that gave its name to the city has long since silted up and been covered by buildings. While the area that was once enclosed between the city walls has lost its original character, so that the place where the oldest centre of population was to be found is now completely lost from sight.

Outside this region was Castro da Cola (the Marachique of mediaeval texts). Although it formed part of the territory of Beja, it has been included here for reasons that have to do with the great migration that always takes place in the summer time. Those who come to visit the beaches of Portugal's southern coast will find themselves passing but a stone's throw from this beautiful fortification and therefore have the chance to discover yet another part of the region's Islamic past, without too much of a detour.

S. M.

VII.1 **FARO**

Information: Rua Da Misericórdia, 8, tel: 289 80 36 04.

The following description of Faro at the end of the 5th-b. $6^{th}/12^{th}$ century is provided by the Sicilian al-Idrisi. It seems, because of its brevity, to be symptomatic of a certain decline in the importance of Faro towards the end period of Islamic influence, particularly if compared with the detailed report that he made of the city of Silves. "Santa Maria do Garbe is built on the shore of the Ocean and its walls are bathed by the seawater at high tide. It is of medium size and very beautiful. It has a cathedral mosque, a smaller one and a chapel. Boats frequently dock and set sail from there. The region produces many figs and raisins." With an area of roughly seven hectares enclosed between its walls, Faro was one of the largest cities in Gharb al-Andalus. At that time, the city occupied a peninsula overlooking the lagoon, and long stretches of its walls were completely encircled by the sea. Its port was situated in what is now the square in front of the Porta da Vila and, further to the east, the water covered the area where we can now see the Square of São Francisco.

There is not much that remains of Islamic Faro. The ravages of time and successive rebuilding work do not allow us to do much more than make topographical interpretations and point out the occasional feature of interest. Because of its exceptional quality, the most important of these is undoubtedly the Porta da Vila. The original site of the citadel (on which a modern factory now stands) is known, as is the location of the mosque (replaced by the cathedral after the Christian Reconquest). In addition to the city walls, the streets in the old city respect the original urban layout of mediaeval times. Hopefully results from various archaeological excavations currently in progress will allow more important data relating to the history of Santa Maria do Garbe to surface.

S. M.

Tombstone, 407/1017, Faro Archaeological Museum.

Slate Tombstone, 5th/11th century, Faro Archaeological Museum.

VII.1.a Faro Archaeological Museum

Praça D. Afonso III, tel: 289 89 74 00. Entrance fee. Open: Monday-Saturday: 10.00-18.30.

Housed in the former Convento de Assunção, the Museum was founded in 1894 by Canon Joaquim Pereira Botto, who left us an interesting catalogue about the pieces that were exhibited there at that time. There is a predominance of Roman exhibits, although the collections also include pieces from other periods.

ITINERARY VII *Between the Algarve and the Mountains*

Faro

The Town Gate, Faro.

The museum's reserve collection contains a set of ceramics from the Almohad period, found near the cathedral during the 1930s, although the region's Islamic past is perhaps best evoked by its small but expressive collection of epigraphs.

The collection of five stones inscribed with Arabic epigraphs at Faro Museum come from different points in the Algarve. The most important of these is the well-known plaque that marked the building of one of the towers in the city of Silves in 624/1227, shortly before the city's reconquest. The others are tombstones, one of them being from Odeleite and another from Sítio das Pontes (Salir).

The inscription was found at Silves towards the end of the 19th century, while a ditch was being dug. The inscription marked the building of a tower, according to its text, which states as follows: "In the name of God, the Clement and the Merciful. God bless Muhammad and his family. The building of this tower was ordered by the emir [...] son of [...] Abu Yusuf, the son of the *caliph,* the emir of the faithful. Abu Ya'qub, the son of the *caliph,* the emir of the faithful, Abu Muhammad Abd al-Mu'min Ibn Ali – may God accept his good works and pardon him his bad ones! And this is written in the month of Ramadan the respectable in the year 624." The tombstone from the year 407/1017, found close to Salir some 30 years ago and brought to light by Martim Velho, has the following text inscribed upon it: "In the name of God, the Clement and the Merciful. Ibn Said died on Friday in the month of Rajab in the year 407. May God have pity upon him. He gave testimony that there is no other god than God, the only one, who has no associate, and that Muhammad is his servant and his messenger."

The Convento de Nossa Senhora da Assunção has been classified as a National Monument since 1948.

S. M.

VII.1.b **Town Gate**

Situated inside the arch leading to the walled area of the city.

Built between the end of the 3rd/9th century and the mid-5th/11th century, this monumental surmounted arch is today an integral part of the 18th-century structure of the town gate (Porta da Vila). It is one of the oldest and most impressive constructions of the Islamic period to be seen in present-day Portugal. The *voussoirs* that

ITINERARY VII   *Between the Algarve and the Mountains*
Loulé

form the arch arranged with alternate colours, are similar to those used in classical Andalusian models and follow an identical principle to the one that was used at the Great Mosque of Cordoba.
The Porta da Vila has been classified a National Monument since 1910.

S. M.

VII.1.c Arco do Repouso

Situated between the Largo de São Francisco and the Largo D. Marcelino Franco.

The Arco do Repouso is a monumental gateway opening onto the old town's eastern side. It was completely rebuilt in the 18th century, which makes it impossible to ascertain now whether its design was originally longitudinal or L-shaped. Two watchtowers, probably dating from the Almohad period, complete this unusual structure, which has recently been restored.
A little further to the south, there is a stretch of wall that was once bathed by the tide. Some of its towers with a semicylindrical base in the Byzantine tradition still remain. These probably date to the 5th/11th century, although they were clearly rebuilt at a later stage.

S. M.

Arco do Repouso, Faro.

For Loulé, follow Estrada Nacional No. 125 and head towards Portimão / Loulé, until you reach the junction with the IP1. Continue along Estrada Nacional No. 125-4 (roughly 17 km.).

VII.2 **LOULÉ**

VII.2.a Islamic Loulé

Information: Edifício do Castelo, tel: 289 46 39 00.

Church of San Clemente, detail, Loulé.

ITINERARY VII Between the Algarve and the Mountains
Loulé

Church of San Clemente, Loulé.

Bowl in green and manganese, and vase in partial cuerda seca, from Vilamoura, $4^{th}/10^{th}$ century, Loulé Museum.

All that now remains of Islamic Loulé is the name (*al-'Ulya* - the hill), the layout of the walls, the location of the mosque and little more besides. The walls enclosed an area of roughly five hectares and show that the town played an important role during that period, even though this is not mentioned in written sources. Some other architectural features also underline the importance of the spread of Islam in Loulé, and the memory of that period was later continued with the building of the municipal market, which is a fine example of neo-Moorish Revivalist architecture.

Of particular note are the *tabiyya* or dry-mud turrets seen in the southern area of the old fortification. Next, note the minaret of the city's mosque, over which was built the bell tower of the Church of São Clemente. Although there are iconographical references to the mosque's minaret at Mértola and the foundation stone of Moura's is also known, in Loulé we witness a rare sight: a minaret where the base has remained unchanged until the present day. Such an interpretation is made possible both by the arrangement of the masonry, (which follows an ancient building tradition) the location of the tower in relation to the church and the very fact that the orientation of the church itself is not at all in keeping with established canons.

S. M.

VII.2.b Loulé Museum

Rua D. Paio Peres Correia, next to the Castle walls. Open: Mondays-Fridays: 9.00-17.30; Saturdays: 10.00 -17.30; closed on Sundays.

The Loulé Archaeological Museum is housed in the former governor's residence, a building that was recently restored and which also houses the Municipal Historical Archives. The exhibition, which occupies

ITINERARY VII   *Between the Algarve and the Mountains*
Loulé

Ruin of Cerro da Vila, Vilamoura.

two rooms, is arranged according to a traditional chronological sequence, which begins with the prehistoric period and ends in the modern period.

The Islamic period is represented by the remains found at two archaeological sites in the municipality: Salir Castle (to the north of Loulé) and the Roman ruins of Cerro da Vila (at the well-known resort of Vilamoura). These are predominantly ceramic pieces, although it is also possible to see a group of distaffs used for spinning.

S. M.

For Cerro da Vila, at Vilamoura, head along Estrada Nacional No. 396 towards Quarteira, turn right at the crossroads leading to Vilamoura and continue on to Cerro da Vila (roughly 13 km.).

ITINERARY VII *Between the Algarve and the Mountains*
Vilamoura

Ruin of Cerro da Vila, Vilamoura.

VII.3 **VILAMOURA**

VII.3.a **Ruins of Cerro da Vila**

Avenida Praia da Falésia, Vilamoura, tel. 289 31 21 53.
Entrance fee. Open: 9.30-12.30 and 14.00-18.00.

This archaeological site has been known since the last century, and its systematic excavation began little more than 30 years ago, when the building of the great Vilamoura tourist complex was first started. Since then, a substantial part of a Roman villa has been unearthed, which clearly remained inhabited until the period of the *Caliph*s ($4^{th}/10^{th}$-$5^{th}/11^{th}$ centuries).
The mosaics and the remnants of what were once imposing Roman baths are the most visible aspects of this carefully pre- served archaeological site. Islamic influence is seen in the artefacts collected from various trenches and ditches, which are currently on display at the Loulé Archaeological Museum, as well as at the Vilamoura Archaeological Centre. Cerro da Vila is also a beacon site for Islamic archaeology in Portugal. It was here, initially, that attention was directed to the evidence of mediaeval occupation at a Roman site. Also it was here that the first systematic study was made of a collection of Islamic ceramics, which, besides a number of luxurious green and manganese and *cuerda seca* pieces, also contains popular locally made pieces. Amongst the latter pieces, artefacts from the archaic tradition predominate, decorated with a reticulated geometrical pattern with a white or red *engobe* or slip. A special mention should also be made of the glazed bowls, which are thought to be $4^{th}/10^{th}$

and 5th/11th-century pieces and a most significant part of this collection.
The ruins of Cerro da Vila have been classified as a Site of Public Interest since 1977.
S. M.

Drive back to Estrada Nacional No. 396 and head towards Loulé. Continue as far as the crossroads with Estrada Nacional No. 124, at Barranco do Velho, and then turn left and head for Salir.

VII.4 SALIR

VII.4.a Fortified Settlement

Information: in the castle, in Loulé, tel.: 289 46 39 00.

A short distance to the north of Loulé is the ancient settlement of Salir. Built on a small, fortified hill overlooking a fertile valley, it still contains some clearly identifiable remnants from its Islamic past. Besides a series of recently excavated housing structures, this period is clearly represented by five *tabiyya* turrets, built on military lines and dating from the Almohad period. Not only does its typology suggest this interpretation, but the outside faces of the walls also display the typical whitewash paintwork imitating large masonry blocks. The absence of a citadel and the relatively small area contained between the walls encourages the view that Salir was a community-type village, serving as a shelter or refuge for peasants who spent their days working in the surrounding fields.

Walls, Salir.

ITINERARY VII *Between the Algarve and the Mountains*
Castro da Cola

A tombstone from the Islamic period was found in the vicinity of Salir, which can now be seen at the Infante D. Henrique Archaeological Museum, in Faro.

S. M.

For Paderne, return to Estrada Nacional No. 124 and head towards Benafim / Alte. On arriving at Portela de Messines, turn left towards Albufeira until Paderne. As you enter the town, you should turn right towards Fonte, and from here follow the dirt track that can be seen on your left.

For Castro da Cola, follow Estrada Nacional No. 124 until you reach São Bartolomeu de Messines, continue along the IP1 towards Lisbon and turn off this road shortly before Ourique at Castro da Cola.

VII.5 **CASTRO DA COLA** (option)

VII.5.a **Excavated Ruins of the Fort**

Information: City Hall of Ourique, tel: 286 51 00 30.

The ancient settlement of Castro da Cola, which has been classified as a National Monument since 1910, is found a few kilometres to the south of Ourique. The site is signposted from the IP1 and it is part of the Cola Archaeological Itinerary, comprising a series of archaeological sites from various periods, of which the *castro* (pre-Roman fort) itself is the major highlight.

Frequently mentioned by a variety of scholars since the late 16th century, Castro

Castro da Cola.

ITINERARY VII *Between the Algarve and the Mountains*
Castro da Cola

Castle, general view, Paderne.

da Cola (the Marachique of mediaeval texts) earned the attention of André de Resende, D. Frei Manuel do Cenáculo and José Leite de Vasconcelos. It was, however, the archaeologist Abel Viana who embarked on a programme of site excavations in 1958, which was only interrupted by his death in 1964. Amongst the features dating from the Islamic period would seem to be the (much rebuilt) perimeter wall, the houses excavated by Abel Viana, and the cistern that supplied the settlement with water. Apparently, Cola was a settlement of the community type, without a citadel, and its structure is similar to that found at other sites, such as Salir, Moura or Portel. The burial ground would have been located on the site where we can now see the hermitage of Senhora da Cola, and several tombstones in Arabic are said to have been found here, one of which is preserved at the Museum of Carmo, in Lisbon.

The material that were found here during excavations – and which are currently kept at the Beja Regional Museum – cover a time span stretching from the Emirates period ($3^{rd}/9^{th}$-$4^{th}/10^{th}$ centuries) to the Almohad period, although it is known that the *castro* had already been inhabited since Neolithic times. Several architectural features (such as the castle's entrance arch, which has been partially dismantled) point to the continued occupation of the Castro da Cola after the Christian Reconquest.

Castro da Cola continues to be a particularly lively place to visit in September each year, when the festivities that are part of a longstanding religious pilgrimage are held there.

S. M.

Drive back to the IP1 and head towards Albufeira. Then take Estrada Nacional No. 124 to Portela de Messines and continue along Estrada Nacional No. 395 until you reach the crossroads leading to Paderne.

ITINERARY VII *Between the Algarve and the Mountains*
Paderne

Castle, Paderne.

VII.6 **PADERNE**

VII.6.a **Castle**

The castle is 2 km. to the south of Paderne.

Information: Rua 5 de Outubro, in Albufeira, tel.: 289 58 52 79.

Paderne Castle is an imposing *tabiyya* fortification built along military lines in the Almohad period and situated little more than 10 km. to the north of Albufeira in the heart of the Algarve Barrocal region. The rocky outcrop on which it was built, and in view of the fact that the Ribeira de Quarteira surrounded it, made Paderne a difficult place on which to lay siege.

The enclosed area, which measures little more than 1,000 sq. m., still protects a lengthy section of its red-earth walls. Of particular interest in the north east section is the L-shaped gateway and the square watchtower connected to the main section by a passageway. Inside the fortification are 16th-century ruins of the chapel of Nossa Senhora do Castelo (whose original construction probably dates back to the 14th century) and the opening of a cistern close to the south wall.

There is a reference made to Paderne in the *Crónica da Conquista do Algarve* (Chronicle of the Conquest of the Algarve): "this town of Paderne has moved to that place that is now called Albufeira, however the other town is still inhabited and protected by its castle and has a very good cistern inside". This statement leads us to suppose that, after the Reconquest, the area must have entered into a period of prolonged decline. We find further reference to the town and its decline in a text by Henrique Sarrão in the late 16th century: at that time, the castle was said to be "uninhabited and devoid of people".

The state of isolation to which the town had been condemned for centuries was finally interrupted a few years ago with the building of the Via do Infante, the major road which passes very close to the castle.

Paderne Castle has been classified as a Building of Public Interest since 1971.

S. M.

Take the Estrada Nacional No. 395 to Albufeira.

VII.7 ALBUFEIRA

VII.7.a Albufeira Archaeological Museum

Praça da República, 1.
Entrance fee. Open: 9.00 12.30 and 14.00-17.30; closed on Mondays.

All that now remains of the Islamic period in Albufeira is its name, immediately suggesting the existence of an inlet from the sea, which has since been eliminated by modern building work.

Certainly for many years prior to its Islamic settlement and because of its strategic position, the town was an important sea port and trading centre for merchants from all over the Mediterranean. Despite its earlier importance, the area once contained between its walls has now been replaced by modern developments. The local museum does, however, have some interesting exhibits testifying to the town's historical past.

S. M.

ITINERARY VIII

Silves: The Capital of Almohad Art

Santiago Macias, Cláudio Torres

VIII.1 SILVES
    VIII.1.a Castle and Walls
    VIII.1.b Silves Archaeological Museum

VIII.2 MONCHIQUE
    VIII.2.a Serra de Monchique

VIII.3 PORCHES (option)
    VIII.3.a Chapel of Nossa Senhora da Rocha

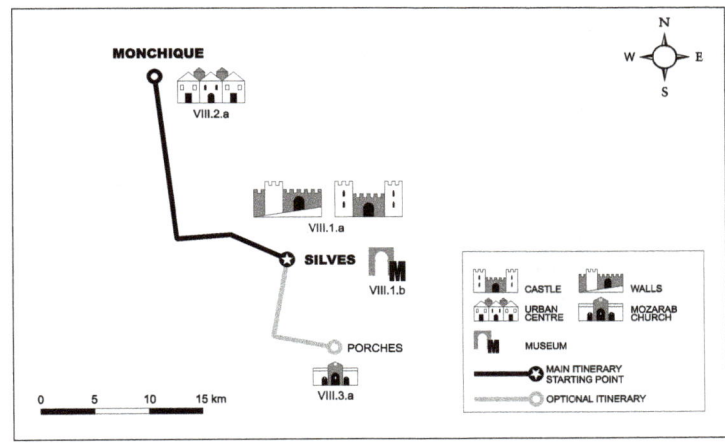

Description of Silves by al-Idrisi, in G. Domingues, Lisbon, 1945.

References to the territory of Silves were scarce until the 4th/10th century. Mention of it became more frequent thereafter and underlines the growing importance of this city by the River Arade, which soon began to exercise clear supremacy over the whole of the western region of the Algarve. According to the description made by al-Himyari, "its territory comprises vast plains and lowland areas and a great mountainous chain of high peaks, where there is an abundance of pastureland and running water. The tree that grows there in greatest quantity is the apple-tree that produces remarkable fruits giving off a perfume similar to that of sweet peas [...] The people from the countryside around Silves are very generous and, in this regard, there are none who can surpass them". Al-Idrisi also drew attention to another resource that was to prove of great importance in this essentially maritime region: "The surrounding mountains [of Silves] produce a considerable quantity of timber that is exported to far-off places".

The Silves of Islamic times stood at a crucial point on a major communication route. This route, originating in Seville and Niebla (in Spain), ran along the whole Algarve coast through Cacela, Tavira and Santa Maria do Garbe, as far as the westernmost point where there once stood the famous old centre of pilgrimage, the Igreja do Corvo.

The city of Silves enjoyed its first brief period of prominence by becoming a refuge for military leaders defeated during the rebellions of 157/774. In the 3rd/9th century, during the first *fitna*, Silves does not seem to have witnessed any special rebellions and remained under the control of the Banu Bakr family from Ossónoba. It was, in fact, this latter city where the representatives of the emir's power were based. Although there are several known references to the *Taifa* Kingdom of Silves in the mid-5th/11th century, and notwithstanding the consulate of the famous governor and poet Ibn Ammar, it was really only in the 6th/12th century that this region reached its most important turning point. From a place of secondary importance, it suddenly became a city of such influence that it was soon regarded as the real capital of the southern region of the Gharb. Its Golden Age, reached under the rule of the Abbadids, continued into the following centuries, as is borne out most exuberantly by the archaeological work currently being conducted at the city's castle. Between the period of Abbadid domination and the end of the process of Islamicisation in the Gharb, in the mid-7th/13th century, the region was subjected to almost constant rebellions and periods of unrest. Only the Almohads were able to exercise any form of effective control over the region, from 548/1154 to 610/1214. The main rebellion was that led by Ibn Qasi. Originating from a *muwallad* family from the territory of Silves, he spent much of his youth studying the Muslim theologians and preaching a life of asceticism. He even commissioned the building of a hermitage in the area surrounding Silves, to which he withdrew with his group of disciples, known as *muridines* (or novices).

The atmosphere of unrest that prevailed in the Gharb at that time was indeed favourable to the ambitious designs of Ibn Qasi, who was engaged in important activity throughout the whole region from 539/1145 onwards. Ibn Qasi's political and religious career came to a sudden end in 546/1152, when he was assassinated in Silves.

ITINERARY VIII *Silves: The Capital of Almohad Art*

Chapel of Nossa Sehnora da Rocha, Porches.

This city played an increasingly important role in the extreme south of the Gharb. After being attacked and conquered by D. Sancho in 584/1189, it came under the control of Ibn Mahfush in 627/1230, with the western region of the Algarve the last bastion of Islam in Gharb al-Andalus.

The Algarve was conquered in two distinct phases: first the eastern region (the Sotavento) and later the western region (the Barlavento). More than just simply the isolated skills of one military leader or another, the major factors behind this resistance were the wealth and dense population of the territory of Silves, as these qualities dictated the need for laborious negotiations and agreements. The military campaigns of the Knights of the Order of Santiago are described in a magnificent text belonging to the Tombos Velhos da Cidade de Tavira (Old Archives of the City of Tavira), which gives a full account of the skirmishes, advances and retreats that took place. Silves was heavily supported by a group of other

ITINERARY VIII *Silves: The Capital of Almohad Art*

Silves

Castle and urban residential centre, Silves.

smaller towns, about which we do not yet have sufficient information to describe their state of development during the Islamic period. Monchique, Alferce (the Castle of Monteagudo referred to in Arabic sources?), Algoz or Alcantarilha are included amongst a group of sites where archaeological discoveries or the simple place-name testify to the role that they played during the period. In other cases, the reports of their conquest or even the presence of fortified walls, provides clear evidence of the importance that these places enjoyed. This was the case, for example, with such fortifications as Aljezur (see Itinerary IX), Alvor and Castelo Belinho, with the last of these still retaining some of its *tabiyya* walls. All that now remains of the towers that were once to be found at Estombar (the Torre de Aben Abece or Abasse) and Porches are their names.

The splendid resources enjoyed by the region of Silves – the famous vegetable gardens and orchards of almond-trees, figs and grapes. The running water, forests of Monchique, the pastureland of Fóia and Picota – turned this area into a kind of garden of delights in sharp contrast to the stormy seas that could be seen beyond the Cape of the Algarve, more recently renamed Cape St. Vincent.

This historical and cultural complex has continued to exist to the present day, at least in part. The small groves of chestnut trees and oaks that are still to be found around Monchique are the remains of a forest that for many centuries provided the wood needed by the Algarve ship-building industry. After a period of sporadic development, during which it intensified its contacts with the western Mediterranean ports (Genoa, Amalfi, Tunis or Seville), the city of Silves passed through various periods of decline and splendour. However, it has never lost the aura and prestige that it enjoyed as an intellectual centre leaving an indelible mark upon the cultural life of Gharb al-Andalus.

S. M.

VIII.1 **SILVES**

Information: Rua 25 de Abril, 26 a 28, tel.: 282 44 22 55.

The following panegyric of Silves delivered by al-Himyari clearly demonstrates the importance that the city had acquired by the end of the Islamic period:

ITINERARY VIII   Silves: The Capital of Almohad Art

Silves

"This city lies to the south of Beja [...] Silves is encircled by a solid wall and has plantations and orchards in its surrounding area. The inhabitants are provided with drinking water by the river, which bathes Silves on its southern side and moves the city's mills situated on its banks. The sea is three miles to the west of Silves. There is an anchoring place on the river and a yard for ship building.
In itself, the city is beautiful to look at, with elegant buildings and some well-stocked bazaars. Like the people from the neighbouring towns and villages, its inhabitants are Arabs originating from the Yemen and other regions of Arabia. They speak a very pure form of Arabic, express themselves in an eloquent fashion and recite verses by heart. All of them, common people and burghers alike, are remarkably gifted."
Earlier, the references made to the city in written sources amounted to a report of the naval battle fought nearby between the Norman "drakkars" and a fleet from Seville, and little more. However, from the $5^{th}/11^{th}$ century onwards, as Faro began to take on a more secondary role, the city by the River Arade assumed greater importance and gradually became the main city in the Algarve.
Until recently, all that was known of Silves in Islamic times was the perimeter of the town walls and the odd piece of archaeological information. Apart from this, the memory of the period of Islamic influence amounted to fleeting references to the names and works of Ibn Ammar, Ibn Qasi and al-Mu'tamid.

S. M.

VIII.1.a Castle and Walls

Entrance fee. Open daily: 9.00-17.00 (October-January); 9.00-18.00 (February-March); 9.00-20.00 (June-September).

The town walls enclose an area of seven hectares, making this the most beautiful military monument in Portugal remaining from the Islamic period. The *tabiyya* walls are in a reasonable state of preservation, whilst the square watchtowers and the red masonry of the citadel give this fortification a quite unique appearance.
A stone now preserved at Faro Museum, which marked the building of a tower (*burj*) in 624/1227, came from this enormous structure. It is quite probable that this new tower may have been a watchtower designed to reinforce the defense system of the city at a time when this was considered to be particularly important. As in Mértola, archaeological work has discovered a substantial part of Silves'

Castle, Silves.

ITINERARY VIII   *Silves: The Capital of Almohad Art*
Silves

Cistern, 6th/12th-7th/13th century, Silves Archaeological Museum.

Islamic past. Both in the citadel, and at various points within the city's historical centre (particularly in the area of Arrochela), important residential structures have been discovered from the Almohad period. Furthermore, the tank that supplied the city with water, which was still in use until quite recently, has been deactivated and is now open to visitors. Popularly known as the Moorish Cistern, this was built in the mid-5th/11th century, although it probably underwent further alterations at a later date. Another structure belonging to the city's water supply – the cistern of the Silves Archaeological Museum (see below) – was excavated and restored during the 1980s and can also be visited.

S. M.

VIII.1.b **Silves Archaeological Museum**

Rua da Porta de Loulé, 14, tel.: 282 44 48 32. Entrance fee. Open: 10.00-18.00 (October-April); 10.00-19.00 (May-September); closed on Monday, 25th December, and 1st January.

The Silves Archaeological Museum was inaugurated in 1989. Built around a cistern from the Almohad period, it houses a collection relating to the local area, displayed chronologically. The most significant section is undoubtedly that which covers the Islamic period, represented by a wide variety of domestic artefacts, used in the most varied aspects of daily life. Quite apart from two capitals from the period of the *Caliph*s, originating from the

ITINERARY VIII   *Silves: The Capital of Almohad Art*
Monchique

city and belonging to the National Archaeological Museum, there are some other treats in store for the visitor. The most interesting pieces, either discovered in archaeological excavations or donated to the museum, are the mouth of a well, an apotropaic plaque and a small glass bottle, a quite unique piece in the context of Islamic archaeology in Portugal.
The main exhibit is most definitely the cistern, which served as the museum's emblem and around which the museum building was constructed. The well is a rare piece from the Almohad period, built in stone and surrounded on the outside by a spiral staircase providing easy and direct access to the phreatic waters; each flight of stairs is covered by a small, segmented tunnel vault.
The Silves cistern was classified as a National Monument in 1990.

S. M.

For Monchique, follow Estrada Nacional No. 124 as far as Porto de Lagos, turn right at the crossroads and then continue along Estrada Nacional No. 266 to Monchique (roughly 29 km.).

*The Legend of the Blossoming Almond Trees
One of the best-known Portuguese legends tells us the story of a Nordic princess who was held prisoner by a Moorish king. The king had fallen in love with the princess and ended up marrying her. However, the princess could not disguise the fact that she felt homesick for her native land and, in particular, for the snow that she had been accustomed to seeing in her country.
On the advice of an old poet, the king ordered almond trees to be planted. When these trees flowered in the spring, they were covered in a white blossom and created the illusion that the fields lay hidden beneath a blanket of snow. Thereafter, the sadness disappeared from the princess's heart, so that,*

ever since that time, when the almond trees around Silves come into blossom in the spring, people have been reminded of the snow of the northern lands.

S. M.

VIII.2 **MONCHIQUE**

VIII.2.a **Serra de Monchique**

*Information:
Largo dos Chorões, tel: 282 91 11 89.*

Panorama, Monchique.

159

ITINERARY VIII   *Silves: The Capital of Almohad Art*

Monchique

Chapel of Nossa Sehnora da Rocha, Porches.

The Serra de Monchique, with its pastures always kept moist by the Atlantic breeze and its dense forests of cork-oaks and chestnut trees, may be considered a special microclimate that is a source of incalculable wealth for the whole of the western region of the Algarve. This fact alone makes it easy to understand the significance and long history of its settlement. On its southern slopes, at the Spa of Caldas de Mochique, there is a thermal spring that has been popular since Roman times. The mountain ridges are crossed by an old road, in an area of much older settlements, surrounded by terraces and gardens, there stretches out before the visitor the present-day town of Monchique. On another ridge stands the ruins of the Islamic fortress of Alferce, which served as a watchtower controlling another mountain pass and marking the boundary of the district of Silves.

C. T.

For Porches, drive back along Estrada Nacional No. 266 as far as Porto de Lagos and then follow Estrada Nacional No. 124 to the Portimão crossroads, turn onto Estrada Nacional No. 125, continuing as far as Porches, and then head towards the beach of Nossa Senhora da Rocha.

VIII.3 **PORCHES** (option)

VIII.3.a Chapel of Nossa Senhora da Rocha

Open: 9.30-12.30 and 14.00-17.00

Perched on the edge of a sheer cliff overlooking the sea is the small white Chapel of Nossa Senhora da Rocha. It remains as a place of worship today, having been an important centre of Mozarab pilgrimage during the Islamic period. The main body of the church is quadrangular in shape and is crowned by an eight-sided dome dating from no earlier than the 17th century. The most remarkable feature is the porch or narthex where two columns and two ancient capitals support three semicircular arches. This natural platform seems to have been the site of other earlier constructions and was encircled along the whole length of the cliff by a masonry wall that has since disappeared; gradually swallowed up when the cliff face has fallen into the sea on successive occasions.

C. T.

Chapel of Nossa Sehnora da Rocha, porch, Porches.

ITINERARY IX

The Headland at the World's End

Cláudio Torres, Cristina Garcia, Paula Noronha

IX.1 SAGRES
      IX.1.a Cape St. Vincent

IX.2 ALJEZUR
      IX.2.a Castle

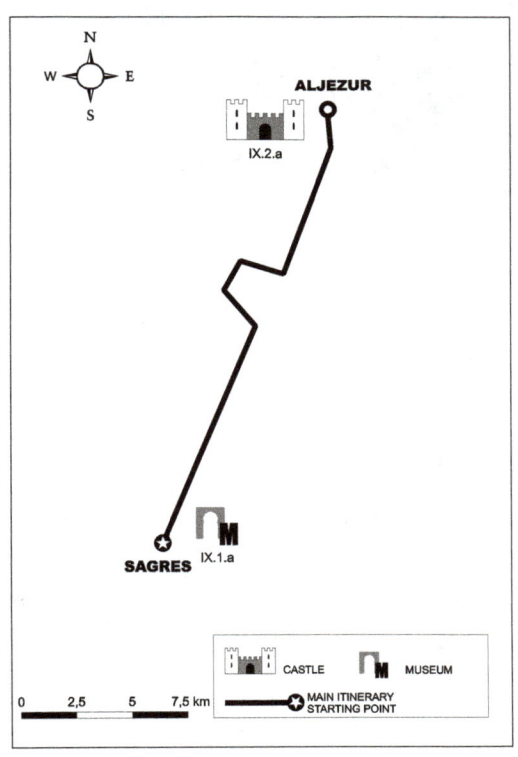

Panorama of the coast, Cape St. Vicent.

ITINERARY IX *The Headland at the World's End*

General view, Cape St. Vicent.

This extremity of the Gharb has always been fairly well populated, both along the coastal strip and in the fertile sheltered valleys further inland. In these south-western territories, the links between the local communities and other ports and peoples seem to be not only more profound, but also more ancient and permanent. The violence and persistence of the north winds that battered the headland of Cape St. Vincent, meant that all sailing boats coming from the Mediterranean, and continuing on to the seas lying further to the north, were obliged to wait sometimes for many weeks until the winds were more favourable. These long waiting periods, during which the crews prepared themselves to confront the rough waves of the great Ocean, led to the development of a complex system of ship building and repair and the rapid sup-

ply of water and other essentials to these ports. The port was a centre of trade and great wealth, with ships docking in and out carrying valuable cargoes. The timbers necessary for building the decks and masts of ships, live animals brought down from the mountain herds, baskets full of figs and dried plums, and wine needed to satisfy the new feeding habits and religious practices that were spreading to the Scandinavian and Baltic countries. All this great circulation of wealth naturally attracted pirates, making it necessary to strengthen the watchtowers built on land and to reinforce the surveillance of the seas, by consolidating fortresses and preparing small fleets of warships to keep predators at bay. And so it was at the western ports of the Algarve, at Lagos, Sagres and Ferragudo, but most of all at Silves, that the great maritime school was

ITINERARY IX   The Headland at the World's End

Sagres

founded. Some centuries later this school would act as the driving force behind the great Portuguese maritime expansion, which first began in these very waters. Not all the inhabitants of this region were Muslims, since an ancient Mozarab tradition linked to the centres of pilgrimage at Senhora da Roca and the Monastery of São Vicente was already established. However, there is no doubt that at the time of its final surrender in the mid-7th/13th century, everyone in the region spoke Arabic, as this was the *lingua franca* for all businesses at that time. A recent analysis of the dialect in this region has detected an abnormal gutturalisation of the "a" sound, which may be attributed to an Arabic influence. This linguistic fact can only be explained as a result of the wholesale permanence and complete integration of the conquered peoples.

C. T.

IX.1 SAGRES

IX.1.a **Cape St. Vincent**

Information: tel.: 282 62 48 73.

In addition to the busy coastal trade originating from Seville and Niebla (in Spain),

Cape St. Vicent.

ITINERARY IX   *The Headland at the World's End*

Sagres

Castle, general view, Aljezur.

there was also a long road that followed the whole of the Algarve coast through Cacela, Tavira, Santa Maria de Faro and Silves. It ended at the westernmost point where there had once stood the Igreja do Corvo (Church of the Crow), a famous centre of pilgrimage in ancient times. In fact this Mozarab shrine was not located on the inhospitable cliffs of Cape St. Vincent, on the site where the lighthouse would later be built. Instead, it was built a few kilometres inland from there. The most meticulous geographer, al-Idrisi, clearly refers to the fact that there was a distance of seven miles between Cape St. Vincent – Taraf al-Urf – and the Igreja do Corvo – Kanisat al-Ghurab. This corresponds in other words to the 13 km. between the Cape and Vila do Bispo or, above all, Raposeira. It would have been in this more sheltered area, where fruits and vegetables grew in abundance, that the monks stored their treasures and tended to the pilgrims' needs.

C. T.

Below, in the words of the 6th/12th century Sicilian geographer, al-Idrisi, is a description of the Igreja do Corvo: "From Silves to the port and village of Halq al-Zawiya [Lagos?], it is a distance of twenty miles. From there to Sagres, a seaside village, it is eighteen miles. From there to the Cabo de Algarve [Cape St. Vincent], which juts out into the Ocean, it is eighteen miles. From there to the Igreja do Corvo [Somewhere between Vila do Bispo and Raposeira] it is seven miles. This church has not experienced any changes since the period of Christian

ITINERARY IX *The Headland at the World's End*
Aljezur

domination. It possesses tracts of land, which the faithful are in the habit of donating thereto, and riches that have been brought by the Christians coming here as pilgrims. It is situated on a promontory that juts out into the sea. On the roof of the building are ten crows, whose absence therefrom has never yet been noted by anyone. The priests who serve the church say marvellous things about these crows, but anyone repeating their words would never be believed. Furthermore, it is impossible to pass by this place without partaking of the hospitable meal offered by the church. It is an obligation, a custom which is never missed and to which people have grown used, as it is indeed an ancient ritual, handed down from one age to another as a result of an age-old practice.

The church is served by priests and monks. It possesses great treasures and very considerable revenue, particularly from the lands that have been bequeathed to it in different parts of the Gharb. These riches are used to satisfy the needs of the church, as well as those of its servants and of all those that are in some way connected therewith, and the needs of those who come here to visit in greater or lesser numbers."
(*Description de l'Afrique et de l'Espagne.*)

For Aljezur, take Estrada Nacional No. 268 heading towards Vila do Bispo, as far as the Alfambras crossroads. From here take Estrada Nacional No. 120 to Aljezur (roughly 45 km.).

IX.2 **ALJEZUR**

IX.2.a **Castle**

Information: Largo do Mercado, tel: 282 99 82 29.

In the Islamic period, Aljezur was a peninsula – as is suggested by its Arabic name – surrounded by a maritime lagoon that was certainly rich in both fish and shellfish. Its extremely fertile land and marshy areas justified the existence of a

Castle, east elevation, according to DGEMN's drawing, Aljezur.

ITINERARY IX *The Headland at the World's End*

Aljezur

Castle, tower, Aljezur.

settlement of farmers and fishermen, who inhabited a fortified area on the top of the hill. As well as being a natural refuge in the case of an attack, it would also probably have been used as a granary and collective store.

The area enclosed by the fortifications does not amount to as much as one hectare and, in addition to containing a large cistern, it is divided along the walls into a series of tiny adjoining compartments that do not seem to have been used for housing purposes. From what now remains of the perimeter wall, it is perhaps possible to attribute the north-facing cylindrical tower and the square turret at the southern end to the Islamic period.

C. T.

ITINERARY IX   *The Headland at the World's End*
Aljezur

Nature Reserve of Costa Vicentina
A long rocky coastline, constantly battered by the winds and the Atlantic Ocean, stretches from Sines to Burgau, including the mythical headlands of Cape St. Vincent and Sagres. "There where the starlight falls downwards and disappears, there emerges the proud kinetic cape, the furthest point upon the coast of rich Europe, entering into the salty waters of the ocean, inhabited by monsters". (Avieno, Ora Marítima, *4th century). The Nature Reserve of the South West Atlantic and Costa Vicentina offers a geomorphologic diversity of sheer escarpments. It stands high above the sea with long sandy beaches, dunes and islets in a narrow coastal strip that is no more than 2 km. wide, occupying an area of 70,000 hectares.*

Rivers and small streams interrupt this rocky mass from time to time, creating different scenarios in the rich areas of their estuaries. Here otters coexist with genets and weasels, the waters are a breeding ground for rock-bass, gilthead fish and flounders and the human presence has transformed the countryside into rice paddies and fields of rain-fed and irrigated crops. But what gives this Nature Reserve its special character is the great scientific value of the different species of flora and wildlife. Some of the flora is absolutely unique to the area, such as the Cistus palhinhae, *the wax myrtle and the service-tree. The migratory birds that nest on the cliffs and islets are also spectacular, in particular the smooth-backed kite, the red-beaked chough and the rock dove.*

The present-day dependence on the activities of fishing and agriculture date back to the Mesolithic period, when small communities would farm this territory on a seasonal basis, feeding themselves sometimes on molluscs and coastal sea fish, sometimes on game and the crops grown further inland. This is borne out by the testimonies of countless fossilised shells found along the coast.

There are several things that you should make a point to see in Nature Reserve of the South West Atlantic and Costa Vicentina. These are the coastal fortifications of Porto Covo, Beliche and Aljezur, the unusual nests of the white stork perched on the top of isolated rocks in the middle of the sea, the intrepid barnacle pickers and the island of Pessegueiro.

C. G. / P. N.

ITINERARY X

The Castles of the River Sado

Cláudio Torres, Isabel Cristina F. Fernandes, Cristina Garcia, Paula Noronha

X.1 ALCÁCER DO SAL
    X.1.a Castle and Museum Centre

X.2 PALMELA
    X.2.a Castle
    X.2.b Palmela Municipal Museum

X.3 SESIMBRA
    X.3.a Castle

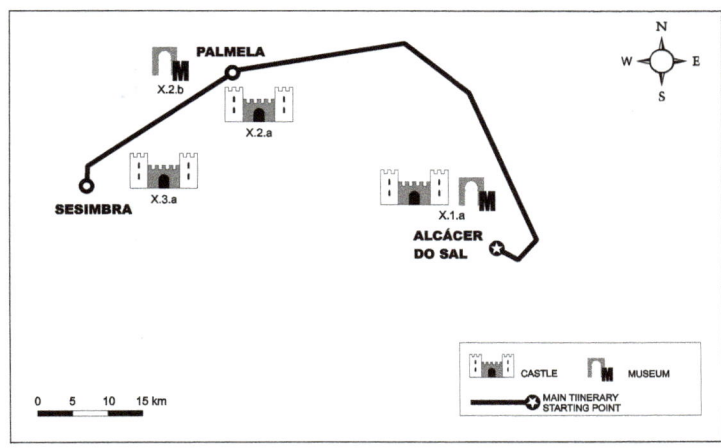

Castle, Palmela.

Alcácer do Sal.

In ancient times, the estuaries of the River Sado and the River Tagus were connected to one another, which meant that the present-day peninsula of Setúbal was an island. According to Greek traditions, as propounded by Avieno in the 4th century, there was at that time, besides the island of Achale or Ácale (the present-day peninsula of Tróia), also another island called Petânion. It is plausible to attribute this island to the area contained between the promontory of Almada, Cabo Espichel and the hills of the Serra da Arrábida and the Serra de Palmela, for in Islamic times it was possible to navigate between the Tagus and Sado rivers by means of the creeks and canals that connected Alcochete to Marateca.
The history of this island, or what was certainly almost an island, is closely connected to the region as a whole, not only through its agricultural production in areas such as the neighbouring marshland of Balata, but also in its wealth as a mining region. The mining of gold nuggets from ancient deposits in the bed of the River Tagus justified the existence of place names such as Almada and Adiça — words that in Arabic have the same meaning as the word mine. Mercury was mined at Coina for many centuries, since it was needed for making gold amalgams. Besides the mining and purification of metal ore, another even more important economic activity was the intense uninterrupted activity of fishing, which explains why the main settlements and fortresses were situated close to areas where there were natural harbours. The fishing of sperm

whales (The sperm whale was caught for the extraction of ambergris) is frequently mentioned, but the area was rich in all types of fish. The ports of the so-called Mar do Palha (Straw Sea – the name given to the lagoon in the River Tagus that lies to the east of Lisbon) such as Almada, Lisbon itself or Coina Velha, as well as the city ports of the River Sado, such as Sesimbra, Palmela and Abudanis, were the main suppliers of all types of fish. Once caught, the fish would be salted and then transported to the territories inland where it was considered as an indispensable part of the local diet.

Because of the Atlantic mists and the fertile alluvium plains, this whole region of the Setúbal peninsula, stretching from the area surrounding Alcácer to the suburbs of Lisbon, was covered by dense forests of stone pines, essential for providing the wooden planks needed for building ships. Large trunks of cork-oak trees were transported down the River Sado and the River Sorraia, their curvature proving ideal for building ships' frames. Much farther away, in the woodland close to the banks of the River Zêzere, trees of solid oak and flexible chestnut were felled and used for the masts of ships. Lisbon, Almada, Palmela and Abudanis were the most important shipbuilding yards in the whole of al-Andalus. The castles of the River Sado formed a system of fortified ports that was quite unique in the Iberian Peninsula, in fact just as extraordinary as the estuary complex that justified their existence and afforded them their livelihood.

C. T

ITINERARY X   *The Castles of the River Sado*
Alcácer do Sal

X.I **ALCÁCER DO SAL**

X.1.a Castle and Museum Centre

Information: Praça Pedro Nunes,
tel.: 265 61 00 40.
Entrance fee. Museum opening times: 9.00-
12.00 and 14.00-17.00; closed on Mondays.

Overlooking the navigable stretch of the River Sado is the majestic fortification Alcácer do Sal (Qasr Abu Danis). In the past, the town was the centre for a vast area of fertile flood plains that became famous in the western Muslim world, both for the woods that surrounded it and for its busy shipyards.

The river was used regularly by countless boats, trading between the bread-producing lands of the upper Sado valley and the other sea ports of the Lisbon region and the present-day Alentejo coast.
In Islamic times, the settlement consisted of two autonomous centres, separated by a majestic crag. Next to the River Sado, classified by al-Himyari as a "great river", was the quarter that essentially fulfilled the purposes of both a port and trading centre. At the highest point, and in a strategically more defensible position, stood the citadel, which was quite substantially altered after the Christian Reconquest.
All that now remains from the last phase of the Islamic period are some turrets in the southern and northern sections of the walls. These were built of *tabiyya* along

Castle, section of mud wall, Alcácer do Sal.

174

ITINERARY X The Castles of the River Sado
Palmela

essentially military lines, and it is still possible in the north-facing area to see the remains of some white-washed paint work designed to imitate large masonry blocks. Although the exact site of the burial ground is not known, the Municipal Museum has in its reserve collection two $5^{th}/11^{th}$-century tombstones, which were found near the castle in the 19th century. The same collection also includes two capitals, which, according to Manuel Real and Ferreira de Almeida, can be attributed to either the end of the period of the Emirs or to the beginning of the period of the *Caliphs*. They can be presumed to have originated from either a palace or some other religious building.

C. T.

For Palmela, follow the A2 motorway in the direction of Setúbal / Lisbon and turn off at Palmela.

X.2 PALMELA

X.2.a Castle

Information, tel: 21 233 21 22.
Open: 10.00-12.30 and 14.00-17.30 (October-May); 10.00-12.30 and 14.00-20.00 (June-September).

The strategic position of Palmela Castle, which was built at the highest point between the Serra da Arrábida and the hills on the right bank of the River Tagus, was to dictate its use and importance right from the very outset. As a military structure, the castle fulfilled the role of both a centre of communication and a point of surveillance. It provided an important base of strategic support in times of war and protected the various routes that linked Lisbon to the regions further south, and the Tagus estuary to that of the Sado. In the Islamic period, and during the Christian attacks in the $6^{th}/12^{th}$ and $7^{th}/13^{th}$ centuries, the castle was a powerful expression of political and military might. It dominated the surrounding area and afforded a clear view of the opposite bank of the river. It looked out over the vast plains of the Ribatejo, taking in the line of hill forts from Coina to Sesimbra, as well as the whole of the Sado estuary.

The few references made to Balmala by Islamic authors are supplemented by Christian sources, particularly the letter written by the English crusader who took part in

Castle, Palmela.

175

ITINERARY X   *The Castles of the River Sado*
Palmela

Castle, Palmela.

the Conquest of Lisbon, known as "Letter to Osberno". He describes how Muslim nobles from Palmela had sought refuge in the city, how the victims of the siege had asked for help and how the castle garrison had been abandoned when Lisbon fell into the hands of the Christians. However, part of the population remained behind and justified the granting of a charter of enfranchisement to the Moors of Palmela by Afonso Henriques in 1170. Some details in the written sources, which have not been clarified, have, however, been investigated archaeologically, with some positive results. Excavations undertaken at the citadel have identified a number of sections of the original wall and a set of residential structures, testifying to successive occupations, restorations, reconstructions and readaptations from the time of the Emirates to the period of the Almoravids ($2^{nd}/8^{th}$-$3^{rd}/9^{th}$ to $6^{th}/11^{th}$ century). The recent discovery of Walls, courtyards, corridors, doors, water channels, ditches, silos, remnants of stucco work and floors made from mortar and clay, remains of food, countless ceramic pieces and fragments, have helped to further illustrate the day-to-day reality of the Islamic presence in Palmela Castle, which lasted for more than four centuries.

Small rural communities, who were forced to pay taxes to the ruling elite based in the castle, were to be found scattered around the surrounding area, with its great expanses of arable land, a region that benefited in particular from an abundance of water and excellent conditions for grazing. Some examples of this form of country settlement are provided by the Muslim village of Alto da Queimada, in the Serra do Louro.

ITINERARY X *The Castles of the River Sado*
Palmela

Recently some archaeological excavations have been undertaken both here, and in other small centres along the ridges of the hills overlooking the fertile valleys of the Corva and Alcube streams.

I. C. F. F.

X.2.b **Palmela Municipal Museum**

The museum is located in the castle's former parade ground.
Open: 10.00-12.30 and 14.00-18.00 (October-May); 10.00-12.30 and 14.00-20.00 (June-September); closed on Mondays.

The Archaeological Museum at Palmela Castle consists of five rooms, four of which include collections and structures from the Islamic period. The museum itself came into being as a result of archaeological work undertaken at the castle's citadel in 1992. As the work was based on an integrated programme, a permanent dialogue was sought between various disciplines, particularly between archaeology and architecture. The constant adaptability required by this partnership resulted in a museological programme

Ceramic Bowl, e. $4^{th}/10^{th}$-b. $5^{th}/11^{th}$ century, Palmela Municipal Museum.

Kitchen ceramics, $5^{th}/11^{th}$-$6^{th}/12^{th}$ century, Palmela Municipal Museum.

ITINERARY X   The Castles of the River Sado
Sesimbra

Capital in Sesimbra Castle, 3rd/9th-4th/10th centuries, Palmela Municipal Museum.

characterised by the compromise between functionality, ease of interpretation and the capacity for renewal. Seen from this perspective, the archaeological museum will remain subject to change, depending on the evolution of field work and laboratory research. With the discovery of residential structures, ditches, silos and the remains of the old wall inside some of the rooms, it was considered useful to leave these exposed, exhibiting them alongside household objects found in other settings. The collection consists essentially of examples of kitchen and tableware from the various phases of the Muslim presence at the castle, as well as other utensils and architectural features.

I. C. F. F.

Leave Palmela by the Estrada Nacional 379 leading to Sesimbra. Access to the town is via a municipal road leading down the hill from the village of Corredoura.

X.3 SESIMBRA

X.3.a **Castle**

Information: Largo da Marinha, 26-27. Tel: 21 223 57 43.

Castle, Sesimbra.

ITINERARY X *The Castles of the River Sado*
Sesimbra

Just like the nearby town of Alcácer do Sal, Sesimbra also consisted of two perfectly autonomous urban centres. Unlike the former Roman town of Salacia, though, where an escarpment of only a few dozen metres separated the walls of the *medina* from the more recently built riverside houses, the old fortified settlement of Sesimbra was located several hundred metres from the riverside village. In the late Middle Ages, and certainly still in Islamic times, the fortification of Sesimbra had both a topography and residential area that were similar to those found at the fortresses of Palmela and Almada. Both also had coastal quarters inhabited by fishermen and sailors with an area of 4 hectares surrounded by an 800-m. perimeter wall and a distant port area.

C. T.

Castle, Tower of Homage, Sesimbra.

Sado Estuary Nature Reserve
A short distance from the city of Setúbal, where the River Sado flows into the Atlantic Ocean, there are 23,000 hectares of river, mudflats and marshland, forming an area of rare natural beauty and great ecological importance. This space was awarded a special status in 1980 when the Reserva Natural do Estuário do Sado (Sado Estuary Nature Reserve) was created. It is symbolised by the friendly and likeable dolphin, whose frequent appearances represents one of its greatest attractions.
This vast wetland area houses countless species of birds, amongst which are found the European stilt, the white stork, the waterhen, the kingfisher and the marsh harrier, as well as various species of herons and ducks.
Amongst the mammals to be found here are otters, genets, badgers, mongooses and foxes. The estuary's biological productivity allowed for the establishment of human communities that have long continued to practise age-old economic activities that are compatible with the preservation of this valuable ecosystem. Examples of such activities are the fishing of red and grey mullet, flounder, sole and gilthead fish, octopus, cuttle-fish and squid. Crustaceans such as crabs and shrimps are also fished here, as are cockles, razor shells and different varieties of clams. The area also produces salt, resin and cork. Acting as a frontier between the estuary and the Ocean, the Tróia peninsula is formed from a string of sand dunes whose stability depends on a vast number of plant species that, because of their characteristics, keep the sand from moving.
On your visit do not miss the small fishing port of Gâmbia, a walk along the moss-covered spit of land, the village of Carrasqueira, with the remains of its fishing port built on stakes stretching out into the water, the bridge at Zambujal made of iron and wood, the Port of Figueiras and the archaeological site at Abul, originally founded by the Phoenicians.

Information Centre: Praça da República, 2900 Setúbal, tel: 265 54 11 40.

C. G. / P. N.

GLOSSARY

Abbadid	Dynasty based in Seville, which governed the south west of al-Andalus between 413/1023 and 482/1090.
Acropolis	Citadel or palatine area built on top of a hill.
Aftasid	Dynasty based in Badajoz, although their influence extended as far as the Lisbon region. The peak of its influence was between 412/1022 and 486/1094.
Alcaide	Until the end of the middle Ages, custodian and defence of a castle or fortress under oath.
Alfiz	Decorative rectangular frame, normally in relief, which surrounds an arch.
Burj	A tower, sometimes surrounded by a secondary wall. The term passed into mediaeval Portuguese toponymy as Alvorge or Porches.
Caliph	From Arabic *khalifa*, meaning the supreme head of the Muslim community in the line of the Prophet's successors. The first *Caliph* of al-Andalus was Abd al-Rahman III, who gave himself the title of the Prince of the Believers in 316/929.
Conventus	Assembly called by the governor of a Roman province to impart justice. Later, the name came to signify the town as well as the district where this activity took place.
Cora	A territorial district that sometimes corresponded to the ancient *conventus*.
Cuerda seca	A decorative process used for ceramics. Before firing and imprinting the desired decorative motifs, a dark line of manganese is drawn around them to separate the various colours of the enamel or glaze.
Engobe	A mixture of non-vitrifiable earth, applied to all or part of a piece of pottery to cover, decorate or outline drawings on it.
Fitna	Literally, "disorder". Term used to designate a period of civil war; in the case of al-Andalus, it corresponds to the period between 401/1010 and 403/1013.
Funduq	Term particular to North Africa to signify a hostel where both pack-animals and men can lodge; a store for merchandise and a commercial centre, analogous to a *caravanserai* or a *khan* in the Islamic East.
Gharb al-Andalus	Western area of the Iberian Peninsula broadly corresponding to the present-day central and southern regions of Portugal.

Glossary

Green and manganese	Decorative ceramic glazing technique where the only colours used are the green of copper oxide and the almost black manganese. At the end of the process, the whole composition is covered with a transparent layer of lead.
Hisn	Castle.
Imam	One who presides Islamic prayer. A guide, chief, spiritual model or cleric, and sometimes also a politician, in a Muslim society.
Iwan	Vaulted hall walled on three sides.
Jihad	Holy war undertaken to protect or defend Islamic territories. Pursued in view of attaining moral and religious perfection. Combat can be engaged in "on God's platform" against dissidents or heathens. *Ijtihad* (same etymology as *jihad*) is the pursuit of a personal interpretation of Islamic law.
Kufic	A form of angular, stylised, often highly decorated, Arabic script used in early Qur'anic, foundation inscriptions and found chiefly in decorative inscriptions; supposedly attributed to Kufa in Iraq.
Madrasa	Islamic School of Sciences (theology, law, *Qur'an*, etc.) and dormitory for students.
Manueline	Style of Portuguese architecture developed during the reign of Manuel I (1495-1521) and characterised by ornate elaborations of Gothic and renaissance styles.
Marwanid	The dynasty that played an important role in Gharb al-Andalus, particularly in the second half of the $3^{rd}/9^{th}$ century.
Medina	Town. In North Africa the old part of an agglomeration created in opposition to the European extension of towns.
Mihrab	Niche in the *qibla* wall, indicating the direction of Mecca toward which worshippers face when praying.
Minbar	Pulpit in a mosque where the *imam* preaches his sermon (*khutba*).
Moorish	In the kingdoms of the Iberian Peninsula, a Muslim converted to Christianity after the Reconquest.
Mozarab	A member of the Christian minorities, tolerated by Islamic right as tributaries and who lived in al-Andalus holding on to their religion and ecclesiastic and judicial organisation.

Glossary

Mudejar	A Muslim allowed to remain among Christian conquerors, without converting, in exchange for a tribute. The adjective also refers to the arts representing handicraft traditions started under Islamic rule and continued for their Christian "customers" following their conquest of a region.
Muladi	A Christian who, during the Arab domination of al-Andalus, embraced Islam and lived among Muslims.
Muwallad	The term applied to those who had converted to Islam. In Gharb al-Andalus, the *muwalladun* (old native families that had become Muslims) played a particularly important economic and political role.
Qaysariyya	Covered market.
Qibla	Direction of the Ka'ba, towards which believers orient themselves for prayer. Wall of the mosque in which the *mihrab* is situated.
Ribat	Fortress built on the border zones, from where religious warriors who dwelled there went to fight the Holy War.
Shaykh	Elderly man respected for his age and knowledge. Tribal chief or brotherhood leader.
Taifa	Each one of the kingdoms into which al-Andalus was divided following the fall of the Caliphate of Cordoba.
Tabiyya	A wall made from mud, which is compressed between caissons. The technique was perfected further in military constructions by introducing lime mortar into the formwork.
Turbet	Mausoleum, tomb.
Villa	(Pl. *villae*.) Large rural property during the Roman period.
Zawiya	Edifice for religious teaching, dedicated to prepare men to become *shaykhs*, which includes the shrine of a saint and built in the place of his birth.
Zellij	Small glazed ceramic tiles used to decorate monuments and interiors.

HISTORICAL EVENTS

92/711	Tariq engages in some early military operations in the Iberian Peninsula.
95/714-97/716	Islamicisation of the western region of the Iberian Peninsula.
99/718	Rebellion of Pelayo in the Asturias.
113/732	Battle of Poitiers.
137/755	Abd al-Rahman seeks refuge in al-Andalus after the massacre of the Umayyads.
138/756-139/757	Beginning of the Ummayad Emirate of Córdoba (Abd al-Rahman I).
145/763-157/774	Rebellion of the Yahsubi tribe, starting in Beja and then spreading across the whole of the Gharb.
148/765-766	Asturian attack on the Miño.
161/778	Battle of Roncesvalles and siege of Zaragoza by Charlemagne.
181/798	Alfonso II of the Asturias advances on Lisbon.
183/800	Charlemagne crowned Emperor of the West.
219-20/835	Building of the Convent at Mérida.
224/839	Exchange of embassies between Córdoba and Byzantium.
	Alfonso II undertakes a series of expeditions into the Viseu region.
228/843-229/844	Norman attack on al-Andalus (Lisbon, Beja, Algarve, Seville).
254/868	Beginning of the *muladi* rebellion against the power of the Ummayads. Their leader, Ibn Marwan al-Jilliqui, founds an independent principality in Badajoz.
	Reconquest of Oporto. Repopulation of the area between the Miño and Douro Rivers by Count Vimara Peres.
264/878	Foundation of Lorvão Monastery.
276/889-90	Death of Ibn Marwan al-Jilliqui.
299/912-300/913	Abd al-Rahman III comes to power.
	Ordoño II takes Évora. Building work begins on the church of Lourosa da Serra.
301/914	Rebuilding of the town walls at Évora.
	León becomes the capital of the Asturias.
316/929	Abd al-Rahman III proclaims himself *Caliph*. Unification of the territory.
324/936	Work begins on the building of the palatine city of Madinat al-Zahra'.
330/942-332/943	War between León and Castile.
343/955	Death of the historian Ahmad al-Razi.
	Sacking of Lisbon at the orders of Ordoño II.
355/966	Norman attacks of the Gharb.
	Death of San Rosendo.
386/997	Al-Mansur attack on Santiago de Compostela.
399/1009-401/1010	Rebellion in Córdoba. Sacking of Madinat al-Zahra'.
403/1013	Emergence of the *Taifa* Kingdoms.

Historical events

412/1012-413/1023	Badajoz, Capital of the Berber Dynasty of the Aftasids. Beginning of the Abbadid government in Seville.
416/1026	Beginning of the Banu Harun domination of Faro. Activity of the philosopher Ibn Hazm.
419/1029-421/1030	Galician rebellion against Bermudo III.
422/1031	End of the Ummayad Caliphate of al-Andalus. Death of the Cacela poet Ibn Darraj al-Qastalli.
425/1034	Reconquest of Montemor-o-Velho by Gonçalo Trastemires da Maia.
430/1039-435/1044	The Abbadids take Lisbon and Mértola.
440/1049	Last *Taifa* Kingdom of the Gharb, in Silves.
441/1050-443/1052	The poet, grammarian, jurist and philosopher Ibn al-Sid is born in Silves. Building of the minaret of the mosque at Moura.
445/1054	The Abbadids conquer Silves.
447/1056-448/1057	Campaign led by Fernando I of Castile against Badajoz. Conquests of Lamego and Viseu.
454/1063-456/1064	Death of the poet and philosopher, Ibn Hazm. Pope Alexander II proclaims the First Crusade in the Iberian Peninsula. Conquest of Coimbra.
462/1070	Beginning of the Almoravid expansion in the Iberian Peninsula. D. Pedro is elected bishop of Braga.
465/1073-471/1079	Death of the historian, Ibn Hajjan. Monasteries of León formed under the auspices of Cluny.
472/1080-473/1081	Death of the poet, jurist and theologian, Abu al-Walid al-Baji, from Beja. Burgos Council (adoption of the Roman Rite).
475/1083	Death of the poet, Ibn Ammar, from Silves. Alfonso VI conquers Toledo, which is thereafter governed by Sisnando.
478/1086-479/1087	Defeat of Alfonso VI by the Almoravids at Zalaqa. Betrothal of Raimundo to Urraca, daughter of Alfonso VI.
482/1090-484/1092	The Almoravid leader Yusuf Ibn Tashfin lays siege to Toledo. Death of Sisnando.
485/1093-488/1095	End of the *Taifa* Kingdom of Badajoz at the hands of the Almoravids, who also reconquer Lisbon. Raimundo governs the territory between the Miño and Mondego Rivers. Death of al-Muʻtamid, king and poet.
489/1096	Marriage of D.ª Teresa to D. Henry of Burgundy. Foundation of the Portucalense Earldom. Henry governs the territory to the south of the River Miño.

Historical events

500/1107	Death of the poet, Ibn al-Milh, from Silves. Almorávid victory at Uclés.
	Death of Raimundo.
504/1111	Almorávid domination of Badajoz, Évora, Lisbon, Santarém. Attack on Oporto.
	Royal charter awarded to Coimbra.
505/1112	Death of Count D. Henry.
510/1117	D.ª Teresa declares herself Queen.
514/1121-516/1123	Beginning of the Almohad Movement in Morocco.
	Death of the poet, Ibn Sara, at Santarém.
	D. Afonso Henriques arms himself a knight.
520/1127-522/1128	Death of the poet and philosopher, Ibn al-Sid, from Silves.
	D. Afonso Henriques is victorious at the Battle of São Mamede.
531/1137-533/1139	Death of Avempace, from Beja.
	Treaty of Tuy. Battle of Ourique.
537/1143-539/1145	Death of Ali Ibn Yusuf. Second *Taifa* Kingdom in the Gharb.
	Rebellions led by Ibn Qasi (Mértola), Ibn Wazir (Évora) and Ibn-Mundhir (Silves).
	D. Afonso Henriques is recognised King at Zamora Conference.
541/1147	Almohad conquest of Marrakesh and Seville.
	Death of the poet, Ibn Bassam, from Santarém.
	D. Afonso Henriques conquers Santarém and Lisbon.
542/1148-545/1151	Building work on the Town Walls in Évora.
545/1151	Agreement signed between D. Afonso Henriques and Ibn Qasi.
	Ibn Qasi assassinated by the people of Silves.
	Failed attempt to conquer Alcácer do Sal.
547/1153-548/1154	Completion of the work of the geographer, al-Idrisi.
	Foundation of Alcobaça Abbey.
550/1156	Almohad's reunification of the southern territories.
553/1159-555/1160	Construction starts on the Lisbon Cathedral and the Templars' Castle at Tomar.
558/1163	Abu Ya'qub Yusuf's rise to power.
560/1165	Birth of the mystic, Ibn Arabi.
	Conquest of Évora and other towns by Geraldo Sem Pavor.
564/1169	D. Afonso Henriques is taken prisoner at Badajoz.
565/1170	Probable date for the remodelling of the Mosque at Mértola.
	Royal charters awarded to the emancipated Moors of Lisbon and other towns to the South.
567/1172-571/1176	Almohad phase in the building of the mosque in Seville.
	The Order of Santiago is installed in Portugal. Truce between Portugal and the Almohad Yusuf I.
574/1179	A Muslim fleet attacks Lisbon.
	Pope Alexander III recognises Portugal's Independence.

Historical events

579/1184-581/1186	The Almohads attack the Gharb and regain control of most of the regions to the south of the River Tagus. Death of Abu Ya'qub Yusuf, as a result of the attack on Santarém. Death of D. Afonso Henriques, who is succeeded by D. Sancho I. Holy order of Santiago receives as donation Almada, Palmela and Alcácer do Sal.
584/1189	Christian conquest of Silves and Alvor.
585/1190-586/1191	Almohad attack on Silves, Torres Novas, Tomar, Almada, Alcácer, Palmela.
591/1195	Almohad victory at Alarcos. Saint Anthony of Lisbon is born.
592/1196-596/1199	Death of Ya'qub al-Mansur. Death of the philosopher Averroës. War between D. Sancho I and Alfonso IX of León.
598/1202	Urban rebellion in Oporto.
607/1211	D. Afonso II succeeds to the throne. Parliament meets in Coimbra.
608/1212	End of the Almohad domination of al-Andalus. Battle of Navas de Tolosa, ending in defeat for the Muslims.
613/1217	Alcácer is definitively taken from the Moors.
619/1223-622/1226	Beginning of the reign of D. Sancho II. Conflicts between the nobles at court.
624/1227	Construction of a tower in the walls of Silves.
627/1230-631/1234	Ibn Hud defeated at Jerez and Mérida. Beginning of the Nazari Dynasty. Conquest of Mérida, Badajoz, Juromenha, Serpa, Moura, Beja and Aljustrel.
633/1236-634/1237	Muhammad Ibn Yusuf Ibn al-Ahmar declares Granada the capital of the Nazari Emirate. Work begins on building the Alhambra. Conquest of Córdoba.
635/1238-639/1242	Death of Ibn Arabi in Damascus. Conquest of Mértola, Cacela, Tavira, Alvor and Paderne.
645/1248	Fernando III takes Seville. D. Afonso II conquers Faro, marking the end of Islamic rule in Gharb al-Andalus.

FURTHER READING

AL-IDRISI, *Description de l'Afrique et de l'Espagne*, ed. R. Dozy and M. de Goeje, Amsterdam, 1969 (reprinting ed. of 1866). Partial Spanish version of this one: *Geografía de España*, Valencia, 1974.

AL-IDRISI, *Descripción de España*, translation D. J. A. Conde, Madrid, 1980 (facsimile ed. of 1799).

ALMEIDA, C. A. Ferreira de, "Arte islâmica em Portugal", in *História da Arte em Portugal*, vol. II, Lisbon, 1986.

ALVES, A., *O meu coração é árabe - a poesia árabe*, Lisbon, 1991.

ALVES, A., *Al-Mu'tamid - poeta do destino*, Lisbon, 1996.

ANACLETO, R., *Arquitectura Neo-Medieval Portuguesa*, 2 vols., Lisbon, 1997.

ARAÚJO, L., "Os muçulmanos no Ocidente peninsular", in *História de Portugal* (managed by J. H. Saraiva), vol. I, Lisbon, 1983, pp. 245-289.

BARCELÓ, C., and LABARTA, A., "Inscripciones árabes portuguesas: situación actual", in *Al-Qantara*, vol. VIII, Madrid, 1987, pp. 395-420.

BARROCA, M., "Do Castelo da Reconquista ao Castelo Românico (séculos IX a XII)", in *Portugália*, vol. XI-XII, 1990-1991, pp. 90-136.

BRITO, Frei Bernardo, *Cronica de Cister*, Lisbon, 1602.

"Carta a Osberno", in OLIVEIRA, José Augusto, *Conquista de Lisboa aos mouros*, Lisbon, Câmara Municipal of Lisbon, 1936.

CATARINO, H., "O Algarve Oriental durante a ocupação islâmica. Povoamento rural e recintos fortificados", in *Al-'Ulya*, review of Historical Municipal Archives of Loulé, 3 vols., 1997-1998.

CATARINO, H., "A ocupação islâmica", in *História de Portugal* (managed by J. Medina), vol. III, 1996, pp. 47-92.

COELHO, A. Borges (organisation, preface and notes), *Portugal na Espanha Árabe*, vols. I-IV, Lisbon, 1972-1975.

COELHO, A. Borges, *Comunas ou concelhos*, Lisbon, 1996.

COELHO, A. Borges, "Lisboa visigótica e muçulmana", in *O tempo e os homens*, Lisbon, 1996, pp. 261-280.

«Cronica do Algarve» and «Tombos Velhos de Tavira», in *Portugaliae Monumenta Historica*, vol. I Scriptores, Lisbon, 1856.

DOMIGUES, J. D. Garcia, "O Gharb Extremo do Ândalus e 'Bortugal' nos historiadores e geógrafos árabes", offprint of *Boletim da Sociedade de Geografia de Lisboa*, 1960, pp. 327-362.

DOMINGUES, J. D. Garcia, *Historia Luso-Árabe*, Lisbon, 1945.

EGRY, A. de, *O Apocalipse do Lorvão*, Lisbon, 1972.

GARCIA, J. C., *O espaço medieval da Reconquista no Sudoeste da Península Ibérica*, Lisbon, 1986.

GLICK, T. F., *Cristianos y musulmanes en la España medieval (711-1250)*, Madrid, 1991.

GOMES, R. Varela, "Arquitectura militar muçulmana", in *História das fortificações portuguesas no mundo* (managed by R. Moreira), Lisbon, 1989, pp. 27-37.

GOMES, R. Varela, and GOMES, M. Varela, "O poço-cisterna almóada de Silves", in *El agua en zonas áridas: arqueología e historia*, vol. II, Almería, 1989, pp. 577-605.

GUICHARD, P., *Structures sociales "orientales" et "occidentales" dans l'Espagne musulmane*, Paris-La Haya, 1977.

IBN HAYYAN de Córdoba [Abu Marwan Hajjan Ibn Khalaf Ibn Hajjan], *Crónica del califa Abdarrahman III an-Nasir entre los años 912 y 942 (al-Muqtabas V) [Muqtabis fi akhbar balad al-Andalus]*, trans., notes and index by María Jesús Viguera and Federico Corriente, Zaragoza, 1981.

LÉVI-PROVENÇAL, É., *La péninsule ibérique au Moyen-Age d'après le "Kitab ar-rawd mi'tar" d'al-Himyari*, Leiden, 1938.

LÉVI-PROVENÇAL, É., "La description de l'Espagne d'Ahmad al-Razi", in *Al-Andalus*, vol. XVIII, 1953, pp. 51-108.

LOPES, D., "Cousas arábico-portuguesas", in *O Arqueólogo Português*, vol. I (pp. 273-279) and vol. II (pp. 204-210), Lisbon, 1986.

LOPES, D., "Os árabes nas obras de Alexandre Herculano", offprint of *Boletim da Segunda Classe da Academia das Sciencias de Lisboa*, vols. III and IV, Lisbon, 1911.

LOPES, D., "O domínio árabe", in *História de Portugal* (managed by Damião Peres), vol. I, Barcelos, 1928, pp. 91-431.

LOPES, D., *Nomes árabes de terras portuguesas* (anthology organised by J. P. Machado), Lisbon, 1968.

MACHADO, J. Saavedra, "Subsidios para a Historia do Museu Etnologico do Dr. Leite de Vasconcelos", in *O Arqueologo Portugues*, vol. V, Lisbon, pp. 51-148.

MACIAS, S., *Mértola islâmica - estudo histórico-arqueológico do bairro da alcáçova (séculos XII-XIII)*, Mértola, 1996.

MACIAS, S., and TORRES, C. (co-ordinators), *Portugal islâmico: Os últimos sinais do Mediterrâneo*, Lisbon, 1998.

MARQUES, A. H. de Oliveira, *A sociedade medieval portuguesa*, Lisbon, 1987.

MARQUES, A. H. de Oliveira, "O Portugal Islâmico", in *Nova História de Portugal* (managed by J. Serrão and A. H. de Oliveira Marques), vol. II, Lisbon, 1993, pp. 117-249.

Memórias Arabo-Islâmicas em Portugal, Lisbon, 1997.

NASCIMENTO, A. A., and BARROCA, M., *Nos confins da Idade Média* (catalogue), 1992, pp. 96-99.

NCIM, *Nos confins da Idade Média. Arte portuguesa dos séculos XII-XV*, Oporto, Lisbon, catálogo, 1992.

OLIVEIRA, J. A. de (translator), *Conquista de Lisboa aos Mouros*, Lisbon, 1936.

PAVÓN MALDONADO, B., *Ciudades y fortalezas lusomusulmanas*, Madrid, 1993.

PICARD, C., *L'Océan Atlantique musulman - de la conquête arabe à l'époque almohade*, Paris, 1997.

PINA, Rui de, *Cronica d'El-Rei D. Duarte*, ed. Alfredo Coelho de Magalhaes, Oporto, 1914.

REAL, M. L., "Inovação e resistência: dados recentes sobre a Arqueologia Cristã no Ocidente Peninsular", in *IV Reuniò d'Arqueologia Cristiana Hispànica*, Barcelona, 1995, pp. 17-68.

SOUSA, J. de, *Vestígios da língua arábica em Portugal*, Lisbon, 1789.

TORRES, C., *Cerâmica islâmica portuguesa*, Mértola, 1987.

TORRES, C., "O Gharb al-Ândalus", in *História de Portugal* (managed by J. Mattoso), vol. I, Lisbon, 1993, pp. 363-415.

TORRES, C., and MACIAS, S., "Arte Islâmica no Ocidente Andaluz", in *História da Arte Portuguesa* (managed by Paulo Pereira), Lisbon, 1995.

TORRES, C., and MACIAS, S., *O legado islâmico em Portugal*, Lisbon, 1998.

VALLVÉ, J., *La división territorial en la España musulmana*, Madrid, 1986.

WILLIAMS, J., *La miniatura española en la Alta Edad Media*, Madrid, 1987.

VITERBO, F. de Sousa, "Occorencias da vida mourisca", in *Arquivo Histórico Portuguez*, vol. V, Lisbon, 1907, pp. 81-93, 161-170 and 247-265.

YARZA LUACES, J., *Beato de Liébana. Manuscritos iluminados*, Barcelona, 1998.

AUTHORS

Artur Goulart de Melo Borges
Licentiate in Archaeology in Rome (Italy). Postgraduate studies in History of art and Museology. He was a Curator at the Évora Museum for twenty years. He has been Director of the Museum for the last five years. He has studied Arabic Language and Culture in the University of Évora and has had a number essays and articles on Arabic Portugal published.

Cláudio Torres
Licentiate in History of Art. Assistant of the Faculty of Arts of Lisbon between 1974 and 1986. Director of the Archaeological camp of Mértola and of the journal "Medieval Archaeology". Director of the Natural Park of the Valle del Guadiana. President of the Administrative Council of the Portuguese National Commission for Monuments and Sites (ICOMOS). Speaker of the Consultative Council of the Portuguese Institute of Architectonic Patrimony (IPPAR). Speaker of the Consultative Council of the Portuguese Institute of Archaeology (IPA). Awarded the Pessoa Prize in 1991. In charge of the organisation of the fourth Conference of Medieval Ceramics of The Western Mediterranean (Lisbon, 1987). Scientific Commissioner in the exhibition "Islamic Portugal. The last signs of the Mediterranean" (Lisbon, 1998).
He is the author of numerous publications, such as: "Portuguese Islamic Ceramic" (1987), "Mertoal's Museum – lapidary nucleous" (in cooperation, 1992); "O Gharb al-Andalus", in "History of Portugal", directed by Jose mattoso (1993), and together with Santiago Macias, O Islão entre Tejo e Odiana *(The Island between Tejo and Odiana,* 1998) and O Legado Islámico em Portugal *(The Islamic Legend in Portugal,* 1998). He also assisted in the "History of Portuguese Art" directed by Paulo Pereira (1995).

Cristina Garcia
Licentiate in Historic Sciences of the Lusiada University of Lisbon. Between 1989 and 1999 she worked in the Ministry of Environment's Institute of Preservation of Nature. Within the programme of ENVIREG (1992) she was the author of the General Plan of the Peninha's Centre of Environmental Education, in the Sierra of Sintra. Within the framework of programmes such as: POA, ODIANA and FEDER (from 1997), she was the author and coordinator of the Intervention Plan of Cacela, in the Algarve. Presently, she works for the Portuguese Institute of Architectonic Patrimony.

Fernando Branco Correia
Official Professor of Medieval History, he also directs archaeological excavations in areas of Islamic settlement. He is also responsible for the Department of Arab and Islamic Studies at the University of Évora, where he teaches. He is also a co-founder of the first Licentiate in History within the specialisation of Arab Studies of Portugal.

Isabel Cristina F. Fernandes
An archaeologist who has participated in a number of projects to investigate Roman and Medieval archaeology, with particular emphasis on the Islamic Period in the Arrábida Peninsula, a field in which she has published several studies.

Maria Adelaide Miranda
Licentiate in History (1975), official teacher (1984) and Doctor in the History of Medieval Art (1996) from the Faculty of Social and Human Sciences of the University of Lisbon. She is the assistant teacher of the Faculty of Human and Social Sciences of the New University of Lisbon. She has also taken part in colloquiums and conferences with interventions regarding the Plastic Medieval Arts.
She has published articles in journals and books, such as: *A Arte da Alta Idade Média. A Arte Românica*, edited by the Open University in 1995, and *A Iluminura de Santa Cruz no tempo de Santo Antonio*, edited by INAPA in 1996. She was commissioner for the exhibition "A Iluminaria em Portugal: Identidade e Influências" and coordinator of the respective catalogue (National Library of Lisbon, 1999). She also contributed to the catalogue for the exhibition: "A imagen do tempo. Livros manuscritos Ocidentais" (Foundation Calouste Gulbenkian, 2000).

Maria João Vieira
Licentiate in Works of Art of the Faculty of Art of Lisbon. Worked for three years in the Ministry of Culture at Green Cape. She has been the cultural patrimony technician for the Town Council of Serpa, since 1992.

Maria Regina Anacleto
Faculty of Arts associate teacher of the University of Coimbra (Institute of Medieval History) Presently her work focuses on neo-classical architecture. In her investigations she has placed special emphasis on Portuguese neo-medieval architecture of the 19th century; and she is the author of various publications on the subject.

Mário Pereira
A teacher of secondary level students, who started his relationship with Patrimony, in the then Portuguese Institute of Cultural Patrimony. For some years he was a collaborator with the IPPAR, and coordinated the thematic exhibition of the Pavilion of Knowledge for Expo 98. He was also President of the commission that installed the Pavilion of Knowledge (from April to December 1999). He is assistant manager of the Portuguese Institute of Preservation and Restoration, and also invitee of academic staff to the ISCTE. He has also published various studies on Cultural Patrimony.

Miguel Rego
Archaeologist. Responsible for the archaeological project of Noudar (Barrancos Council) and associate founder of the Archaeological Camp of Mértola.

Paula Noronha
Licentiate in Landscape Architecture from the Superior Institute of Agronomy of the Technical University of Lisbon in 1998. Her activities are concentrated mainly in the Natural Park of the Ria Formosa. This is a protected area considered a Humid Zone of International importance, where she has specialised in management of coastal and humid areas, especially with concern to the instruments of territorial management. As a professional, she manages projects involved with landscape improvements.

Ruben de Carvalho
A professional Journalist since 1963. He has produced various musicals, and was a commissar of the "Organisation of Lisbon 94 – European Capital of Culture" for the areas of popular music, urban animation and editions. He has been member of the Portuguese Parliament in the seventh legislature (1995-1999).

Santiago Macias
Licentiate in History from the University of Lisbon (1985) and Doctor in Medieval History from the New University of Lisbon (1995). He is presently the Chief of the Socio-cultural Department of the Town Council of Mértola. Researcher of the archaeological camp of Mértola in the areas of History and medieval archaeology. He also coordinates the journal *Medieval Archaeology*. Presently he is responsible for the installation of the Islamic Museum of Mértola. He was a scientific commissar of the exposition: "Islamic Portugal. The last signs of the Mediterranean" (Lisbon, 1998). He has also collaborated with the "History of Portugal" directed by Jose Mattoso (1993) and with the "History of Portuguese Art" directed by Paulo Pereira (1995). He has published *Islamic Mértola* (1996), and together with Claudio Torres: *O Islão entre Tejo e Odiana* (1998) and *O Legado Islâmico em Portugal* (1998).

Susana Gómez
Licentiate in Geography and History and Doctorate in Medieval History from the Faculty of Geography and History of the University Complutense of Madrid. Between 1985 and 1993 she took part in various archaeological excavations and in the conservation of archaeological pieces. Since 1993 she has been a researcher-archaeologist of the Archaeological Camp of Mértola. Between 1993 and 1997 she taught different courses in Museology, History of Art and Archaeology.
She has published works such as: "Decorated Ceramic of Mértola – Portugal (IX to XIII centuries)", in *Actes du VIème Colloque sur la céramique médiévale en Mediterranée*, Aix-en-Provence (1987), "A cerámica do Gharb al-Ândalus", *in Portugal Islâmico. Os últimos sinais do Mediterâneo* (Lisbon, 1998).

ISLAMIC ART IN THE MEDITERRANEAN

This cycle of Museum With No Frontiers Exhibition Trails permits the discovery of secrets in Islamic Art, its history, construction techniques and religious inspiration.

ALGERIA

LEGACY OF ISLAM IN ALGERIA: The Art and Architecture of Light* introduces the varied and richest forms Islamic art assumed in Central Maghreb (Algeria), an important artistic heritage related to crucial events that marked the country's history, from the rise of dissident religious movements to the influence of great dynasties, and the roles played by trade and pilgrimage routes and by the Ottomans in the Mediterranean cities. The synthesis of Arab and Berber, African, Andalusian and Eastern influences shaped the artistic and architectural models, the purity and harmony of Ibadid architecture, Almoravid mosques, Ziyanid monuments and Ottoman palaces on the Mediterranean shore.

Five itineraries invite you to discover 70 museums, monuments and sites in Biskra, Ghardaia, Bani Isguen, Algiers, Tlemcen, Nedroma and Tamentit (among others).

EGYPT

MAMLUK ART: The Splendour and Magic of the Sultans tells the story of almost three centuries of political security and economic stability achieved by the sultans' successful defence against Mongol and Crusader threats. The intellectual, scientific and artistic currents that flourished then are manifest in Mamluk architecture and decorative arts, almost modern in their elegant and lively simplicity, bearing witness to the vitality of Mamluk trade, to their cultural exuberance and to their military and religious strength.

Eight itineraries invite you to discover 51 museums, monuments and sites in Cairo, Alexandria and the Nile Delta.

ITALY

SICULO-NORMAN ART: Islamic Culture in Medieval Sicily illustrates how the great artistic and cultural heritage of the Arabs who ruled the island in the 10th and 11th centuries was assimilated and reinterpreted during the Norman reign that followed, achieving its acme in the resplendent age of Ruggero II in the 12th century. Spectacular coastal and mountain landscapes provide the backdrop for visits to villages, castles, gardens, churches and Christianised old mosques.

Ten itineraries invite you to discover 91 museums, monuments and sites in Palermo, Monreale, Mazara del Vallo, Salemi, Segesta, Erice, Cefalù and Catania (among others).

JORDAN

THE UMAYYADS: The Rise of Islamic Art presents a journey through the great artistic and cultural flourishing that gave birth to the formative phase of Islamic art during the 7th and 8th centuries. The Umayyads unified the Mediterranean and Persian cultures and developed an innovative artistic synthesis that incorporated and immortalised Classical, Byzantine and Sassanid heritage. The elegant architecture of desert castles and the frescoes, mosaics and masterpieces of figurative and decorative art still evoke the strong sense of realism and the great cultural, artistic and social vitality of the centres of the Umayyad Caliphate.

Five itineraries invite you to discover 43 museums, monuments and sites in Amman, Madaba, Al-Badiya, Jerash, Umm Qays, Aqaba and Humayma (among others).

MOROCCO

ANDALUSIAN MOROCCO: Discovery in Living Art tells the story of the exchanges between the furthest frontier of the Maghreb and Al-Andalus for more than five centuries. Political and social circumstances gave birth to a crossroads of cultures, techniques and artistic styles revealed by the splendour of Idrisid, Almoravid, Almohad and Marinid mosques, minarets and madrasas. The influence of Cordoban architecture and Andalusian decorative models, horseshoe arches, floral and geometric motifs and the use of stucco, wood and polychromatic tiles, display the continuous interchange that made Morocco one of the most brilliant homes of Islamic civilisation.

Eight itineraries invite you to discover 89 museums, monuments and sites in Rabat, Meknès, Fez, Chefchaouen, Tétouan and Tangier (among others).

PALESTINIAN TERRITORIES

PILGRIMAGE, SCIENCE AND SUFISM: Islamic Art in the West Bank and Gaza explores a period during the reigns of the Ayyubid, Mamluk and Ottoman dynasties when numerous pilgrims and scholars from all quarters of the Muslim world came to Palestine. The great dynasties commissioned architectural and artistic masterpieces in the most important religious centres. Attracting the most learned scholars, many centres enjoyed considerable prestige and encouraged the spread of a rarefied art that still fascinates today. The Islamic monuments and architecture of this Exhibition Trail clearly reflect the connections between dynastic patronage, intellectual activity and the rich expression of people's devotion, rooted in this land for centuries.

Nine itineraries invite you to discover 70 museums, monuments and sites in Jerusalem, Jericho, Nablus, Bethlehem, Hebron and Gaza (among others).

PORTUGAL

IN THE LANDS OF THE ENCHANTED MOORISH MAIDEN: Islamic Art in Portugal uncovers five inspired centuries of Islamic civilisation that shaped the people of the former Gharb al-Andalus. From Coimbra to the furthest reaches of the Algarve there are palaces, Christianised mosques, fortifications and urban centres, all of which bear witness to the splendour of a glorious past. This artistic recollection is the expression of a very delicate symbiosis that determined the particularities of vernacular architecture and still permeates the cultural identity of Portugal.

Ten itineraries invite you to discover 76 museums, monuments and sites in Lisbon, Sintra, Coimbra, Evora, Mertola, Faro and Sesimbra (among others).

SPAIN

MUDEJAR ART: Islamic Aesthetics in Christian Art uncovers the fascinating richness of a genuinely Hispanic cultural and artistic symbiosis that became a distinctive element of Christian Spain after the end of Arab rule. Mudejars were Muslims who were allowed to stay in the reconquered territories and Mudejar artists and craftsmen strongly influenced the culture and art of the new Christian kingdoms. Beautifully decorated brick-built churches, monasteries and palaces in Aragona, Castile, Estremadura and Andalusia provide a unique example of the creative preservation of Islamic forms within Christian art in Spain between the 11th and 16th centuries.

Thirteen itineraries invite you to discover 124 museums, monuments and sites in Madrid, Guadalajara, Saragossa, Tordesillas, Toledo, Guadalupe and Seville (among others).

SYRIA

THE AYYUBID ERA: Art and Architecture in Medieval Syria* focuses on the unique artistic and architectural development in 12th–13th century Syria, when Atabeg and Ayyubid military resistance to the Crusaders coincided with a great cultural and artistic revival in the most important Syrian cities. The Ayyubid patrons provided educative, religious and charitable institutions; their intense activity left its mark in the sober elegance of mosques, madrasas, citadels, mausoleums and hospitals, embellished with Eastern architectural and decorative motifs, muqarnas, Kufic inscriptions, carved stucco and wooden minbars, beautifully illuminated manuscripts, pottery, metalwork and textiles.

Eight itineraries invite you to discover 95 museums, monuments and sites in Damascus, Bosra, Homs, Hama, Tartus, Aleppo and Raqqa (among others).

TUNISIA

IFRIQIYA: Thirteen Centuries of Art and Architecture in Tunisia is a voyage through the history of the Islamic architecture of the Maghreb, to uncover a millenary civilisation that made works of art of its most important spaces. The great Islamic dynasties – Abbasids, Aghlabids, Fatimids, Zirids, Almohads, Hafsids, Ottomans – and Islamic religious schools and movements left the mark of their artistic expression over the centuries. Islamic art in Tunisia is a cultural crossroads, widely influenced by local artistic customs, by Andalusian and eastern architectural and decorative elements, by Arab, Roman and Berber traditions and by the variety of its natural landscape.

Eleven itineraries invite you to discover 108 museums, monuments and sites in Tunis, Sidi Bou Saïd, Bizerte, Testour, Al-Kef, Kairouan, Mahdia, Sfax, Tozeur and Gabès (among others).

TURKEY

EARLY OTTOMAN ART: The Legacy of the Emirates presents the artistic and architectural expressions in Western Anatolia and the emergence of the Ottoman dynasty in the 14th and 15th centuries. The Turkish Emirates developed a new stylistic synthesis by blending Central Asian and Seljuq traditions and the legacy of the Greek, Roman and Byzantine past. The architectural schemes of mosques, hammams, hospitals, madrasas, mausoleums and the great religious complexes, columns and domes, floral and calligraphic decoration, ceramics and illumination testify to the richness of styles. The cultural and artistic flourishing that matched the rise of the Ottoman Empire was deeply marked by the distinctive legacy of the Emirates.

Eight itineraries invite you to discover 61 museums, monuments and sites in Milas, Selçuk, Manisa, Bursa, İznik, Karacabey, Çanakkale, Gelibolu and Edirne (among others).

---

* Under preparation.

www.ingramcontent.com/pod-product-compliance
Lightning Source LLC
Chambersburg PA
CBHW050243170426
43202CB00015B/2900